The Unitarian Life:
Voices From The Past And Present

Edited by Stephen Lingwood

The Lindsey Press
London

Published by the Lindsey Press
on behalf of The General Assembly of Unitarian and Free
Christian Churches
Essex Hall, 1–6 Essex Street, London WC2R 3HY, UK

© The General Assembly of Unitarian and Free Christian
Churches 2008

ISBN 978-0-85319-076-9

Typeset by Garth Stewart, Oxford

Printed and bound in the United Kingdom by
Lightning Source, Milton Keynes

Contents

Acknowledgements

I am in debt to a number of people for their assistance in the production of this volume, and first among them the members of the *Unitarian Futures* email discussion group, among whom the idea for this book was initially discussed. My thanks are due to George Chryssides, who took the idea to the Lindsey Press and was a source of encouragement in the early months of the work. Jessica Kimmet lent me her computer in the period when I was without one, and most of this book was written on it. Donald Phillips did much of the preliminary work on copyright clearance, and Catherine Robinson took up that task in the later stages of production. This was a huge and necessary job, and I am very grateful to both of them. Catherine also copy-edited the text and co-ordinated the production. The members of the Lindsey Press Panel have supported the project in various ways from beginning to completion. I also want to acknowledge Michael Dadson, who, if I remember correctly, came up with the phrase '*how to live Unitarianly*'.

Finally, my thanks to all the Unitarian communities to which I have belonged around the world. This is my gift to you.

Stephen Lingwood
Manchester, January 2008

Preface

Who are the Unitarians?

The Unitarians are a spiritual community who encourage you to think for yourself. They believe:
- that everyone has the right to seek truth and meaning for themselves;
- that the fundamental tools for doing this are one's own life experience, one's reflection upon it, one's intuitive understanding, and the promptings of one's own conscience;
- that the best setting for this is a community which welcomes people for who they are, complete with their beliefs, doubts, and questions.

They can be called "religious liberals":
- "religious" because they unite to celebrate and affirm values that embrace and reflect a greater reality than self;
- "liberal" because they claim no exclusive revelation or status for themselves; and because they afford respect and toleration to those who follow different paths of faith.

They are called "Unitarians":
- because of their traditional insistence on divine unity, the oneness of God;
- because they affirm the essential unity of humankind and of creation.

History in brief

The roots of the Unitarian movement lie principally in the Protestant Reformation of the sixteenth century. At that time, people in many countries across Europe began to claim:

- the right to read and interpret the Bible for themselves;
- the right to have a direct relationship with God, without the mediation of priest or church;
- the right to set their own conscience against the claims of religious institutions.

Many came to question "orthodox" Christian doctrine and to affirm beliefs of their own. These included:

- the Unity or unipersonality of God, as opposed to the doctrine of the Trinity – hence the name "Unitarian";
- the humanity, as opposed to the deity, of Christ;
- the worth of human beings, as opposed to ideas of original sin, inherited guilt, and innate depravity;
- the universal salvation of all souls, as opposed to the doctrine that most of humanity is predestined to damnation.

The earliest organised Unitarian movements were founded in the sixteenth century in Poland and Transylvania. In Britain, a number of early radical reformers professed Unitarian beliefs in the sixteenth and seventeenth centuries, some suffering imprisonment and martyrdom. An organised Unitarian movement did not emerge until the late eighteenth century. The first avowedly Unitarian church in Britain was opened in Essex Street, London, in 1774. Denominational structures were developed during the 19th century, finally uniting in the present General Assembly in 1928.[1]

For more details about Unitarianism, contact
the Information Department, Unitarian Headquarters,
1–6 Essex Street, London WC2R 3HY, tel. 0207 240 2384;
or visit the General Assembly website at www.unitarian.org.uk

x

Introduction

I am a Unitarian.
I know I am a Unitarian because I find affinity with you.
I am here, now, in fellowship with you.
You are here, there, everywhere.
You are before me, beside me, behind me.
I live the Unitarian way. So do you.
You have lived out your lives; you are as yet unborn.
Be with me, as we teach each other how to be Unitarian.

Kay Millard [2]

This book emerged out of dialogue, the book itself is a dialogue, and I hope it will go on to stimulate more dialogue. The initial exchanges took place in a small email group of which I am a member, called *Unitarian Futures*. We were wrestling with issues such as the nature, purpose, and future of Unitarianism. What is Unitarianism? What should Unitarianism be? How should we better express our religious identity, both to grow deeper within our own faith, and to share our faith more meaningfully with others? It seems that these questions need to be answered if we are to move forward as a religious movement.

Each of us can express what we as individuals believe, but what do we have in common? What can we say that expresses our *communal* religious vision? If we are going to grow as a religious movement, I think we need to communicate our faith and values more clearly. In North America, Unitarian Universalists express their vision with their Seven Principles, but nothing like that exists in Britain. So how do we express the nature of Unitarianism as a religious community?

There are things that we cannot do. We cannot recite a creed, or produce dogma that will stand for all eternity. We cannot produce a document from on high, written by an elite minority and imposed on the people. But perhaps we can "teach each other how to be Unitarian".

Perhaps we can speak to one another about what it means to each of us to be Unitarians. We can engage in dialogue with one another about what Unitarianism means to each of us. And we need not limit that dialogue. We can pay attention to a cloud of witnesses from many different countries around the world and many different times in history. We can delve deep into the traditions of our spiritual ancestors and listen to their voices. In doing so, we can create a "living scripture": a loose, dynamic collection of texts which brings together essential insights from the past and present of our movement.

The idea for this book emerged as a way to express this dialogue, to function as a "work-in-progress-living-scripture", and I was asked to begin working on it. It seemed to me that what was needed was a document that would serve rather as a "Book of Discipline" acts in some religious denominations. However, I did not think it was necessary to produce a definite, accurate description of polity, committees, and governance. Rather what was needed was something expressing the *spirit* of Unitarianism, and the *depths* of Unitarianism. One of the weaknesses of the movement today is that we are not aware of the breadth and depth of our global religious community. I wanted a book that would help us to understand contemporary Unitarianism as rooted in its history, yet moving on into the future in freedom.

So a format emerged: a collection of short contributions from a wide range of Unitarians, arranged thematically. Every contribution in this book is by a Unitarian, or a proto-Unitarian, or a Universalist, or a Unitarian Universalist – or someone very closely associated with Unitarianism, who may never have identified himself or herself as Unitarian, or never belonged to a Unitarian church (for example, Thomas Jefferson). The only exceptions are a small number of ancient scriptural passages which have been included because they express the Unitarian spirit very well and have been valued by Unitarians over the years.

My aims in collecting contributions were to get at least half from people still living, at least half from people in Britain and Ireland,

and at least half from women. I have more or less succeeded in the first two aims, but not the last. I believe that about a quarter of contributions in this book are from women. I do not think this is acceptable. Nevertheless it is somewhat inevitable with a book that is at least partly historical. *The Epic of Unitarianism*, compiled by David Parke nearly fifty years ago, for example, contains no contributions from women. Nevertheless there have been some remarkable Unitarian women, including women ministers, and I deeply regret that I could not find more contributions from more of them. That illustrates why this is a work in progress: recording the voices of Unitarian women, of the past and of the present, is a task that is still incomplete.

Some people may feel that I have missed out some important Unitarian historic figures. Perhaps so, but this is not a history book, surveying Unitarian writing from the past; rather it is an expression of how Unitarians past and present have helped to shape this religious community as it is today. Voices from the past are presented alongside voices from the present. Famous names appear alongside less well known ones. This expresses our affirmation of the inherent worth and dignity of every individual. All voices have value. I have included very short biographical notes at the end of the book, to help to explain the historical and cultural contexts of the contributors.

In some ways I feel it would have been better if this book had been produced by a committee rather than by one person. However, this would have extended the process, and I believed that publishing an initial edition that could be used by congregations and individual Unitarians was more of a priority. I hope that a second edition, or something like it, can be produced some time in the future by a number of people, with a scope that will be broader and more representative.

Nevertheless I hope that my editing has been fair, and that this book offers a broad view of Unitarianism. I have intentionally gathered a variety of viewpoints, not in order to present oppositional antagonistic positions, but in order to ensure diversity. There is little in this book that I would directly disagree with, although there are perhaps some passages that I would want to question, to tease out the meaning of the authors. I have yielded to the temptation to write a couple of contributions myself, but I have done this only where I felt that there was something important to say that no other contributor was covering. I hope that this indulgence does not offend.

The book is arranged in four parts: *The Principles and Values of Unitarianism; Unitarian Diversity; Unitarian Perspectives;* and *How to Live Unitarianly.* These divisions are not rigid, and many passages could have been included in any one of these sections. Nevertheless I think these divisions are useful in helping to define the different dimensions of the Unitarian Life.

So this book is for life-long Unitarians, as well as new Unitarians and those who just want to know more about Unitarianism. It is for those who want to deepen their Unitarian faith, to better understand their Unitarian faith, and to better express and explain their Unitarian faith. It could be read from cover to cover, or it could be dipped into here and there when needed. I hope it can be used for personal reflection and public worship, and as a starting point for dialogue. I hope that this is a book to be thumbed through, written on, and meditated with, not simply read once and put on a shelf. But above all else, this book is a simple invitation to "be with me, as we teach each other how to be Unitarian".

Part I:
The Principles and Values of Unitarianism

What is Unitarianism? Asking this question in Transylvania, you would most likely receive a reply that spoke of "the oneness of God". In the British Isles you are more likely to hear about "freedom, reason, and tolerance". In North America you would hear about "the Seven Principles", the first of which is "the inherent worth and dignity of every person". These answers are not contradictory, but complementary.

Unitarianism is a creedless faith, rooted in the Christian tradition, yet on a spiritual adventure in search of truth, justice, and healing for the world. We are a faith community for those on a spiritual journey, for those who believe there is still more to be discovered in religion. We believe in religious exploration – through the intellect and through the spirit. Through the intellect we explore religious questions in sermons, lectures, workshops, and dialogue. Through the spirit we explore through worship, music, ritual, meditation, and prayer.

Although we are on a spiritual journey, we are not only concerned with our own spiritual enlightenment, but we know that the world today cries out for justice, compassion, and healing. We believe that religion is useless if it does not result in real prophetic and compassionate living in our everyday lives. Therefore our religious journey includes service to humanity and the world.

But what principles and values guide our religious journey as a faith community? Part I explores this question, with contributions exploring our foundational principles: reverence for life; respect for the individual; love; the importance of community; freedom; tolerance; pluralism; dialogue; spirituality; democracy; rational thinking; and prophetic living.

The revised Object of the General Assembly of Unitarian and Free Christian Churches (UK)

We, the constituent congregations, affiliated societies and individual members, uniting in a spirit of mutual sympathy, co-operation, tolerance and respect; and recognising the worth and dignity of all people and their freedom to believe as their consciences dictate; and believing that truth is best served where the mind and conscience are free, acknowledge that the Object of the Assembly is:

To promote a free and inquiring religion through the worship of God and the celebration of life; the service of humanity and respect for all creation; and the upholding of the liberal Christian tradition.

To this end, the Assembly may:

Encourage and unite in fellowship bodies which uphold the religious liberty of their members, unconstrained by the imposition of creeds;

Affirm the liberal religious heritage and learn from the spiritual, cultural and intellectual insights of all humanity;

Act where necessary as the successor to the British and Foreign Unitarian Association and National Conference of Unitarian, Liberal Christian, Free Christian, Presbyterian and other Non-Subscribing or Kindred Congregations, being faithful to the spirit of their work and principles (see appendix to the constitution), providing always that this shall in no way limit the complete doctrinal freedom of the constituent churches and members of the Assembly;

Do all other such lawful things as are incidental to the attainment of the above Object.

Adopted at the General Assembly Annual Meetings, April 2001

Principles of the Unitarian Universalist Association (USA)

We, the member congregations of the Unitarian Universalist Association, covenant to affirm and promote

- The inherent worth and dignity of every person;
- Justice, equity and compassion in human relations;
- Acceptance of one another and encouragement to spiritual growth in our congregations;
- A free and responsible search for truth and meaning;
- The right of conscience and the use of the democratic process within our congregations and in society at large;
- The goal of world community with peace, liberty, and justice for all;
- Respect for the interdependent web of all existence of which we are a part.

The living tradition which we share draws from many sources:

- Direct experience of that transcending mystery and wonder, affirmed in all cultures, which moves us to a renewal of the spirit and an openness to the forces which create and uphold life;
- Words and deeds of prophetic women and men which challenge us to confront powers and structures of evil with justice, compassion, and the transforming power of love;
- Wisdom from the world's religions which inspires us in our ethical and spiritual life;
- Jewish and Christian teachings which call us to respond to God's love by loving our neighbors as ourselves;
- Humanist teachings which counsel us to heed the guidance of reason and the results of science, and warn us against idolatries of the mind and spirit;
- Spiritual teachings of earth-centered traditions which celebrate the sacred circle of life and instruct us to live in harmony with the rhythms of nature.

Grateful for the religious pluralism which enriches and ennobles our faith, we are inspired to deepen our understanding and expand our vision. As free congregations we enter into this covenant, promising to one another our mutual trust and support.

(Reprinted with the permission of the Unitarian Universalist Association)

The Flaming Chalice: Unitarian symbol

The flaming chalice has become the internationally recognised symbol of the Unitarian movement. While originally the image appeared only as a device on letterheads and neckties, the lighting of a chalice is increasingly becoming a feature of communal worship in Unitarian congregations.

History

The philosopher A.N. Whitehead said that real symbols have the power to change history. The history of the chalice symbol is significant. It began by representing the religious courage of Jan Hus, a fifteenth-century Czech priest, who was martyred for offering communion to his congregants in defiance of the Roman church, which reserved the sharing of wine to priests only. He was burnt at the stake for this act, and Unitarians too have a history of being persecuted for innovative and democratic deeds in religion.

During the Second World War an American Unitarian, Reverend Charles Joy, was stationed in Lisbon to help refugees from Nazism escape to safe havens. As executive director of the Unitarian Service Committee he felt that this new, unknown organisation needed some visual image to represent Unitarianism to the world, especially when dealing with government agencies abroad.

He commissioned a Czech refugee and cartoonist, Hans Deutsch, to design something that could be used on official documents, and thus an early version of the modern chalice came into being.

Joy described what Deutsch had drawn in the following terms: "A chalice with a flame, the kind of chalice which the Greeks and Romans put on their altars. The holy oil burning in it is a symbol of helpfulness and sacrifice... This was in the mind of the artist. The fact, however, that it remotely suggests a cross was not in his mind, but to me this also has merit. We do not limit our work to Christians. Indeed, at the present moment, our work is nine-tenths for the Jews, yet we do stem from the Christian tradition and its central theme of sacrificial love."

The American Universalists and Unitarians merged in the early sixties, and versions of the symbol were adopted by the Unitarian Universalist Association and by the General Assembly of Unitarian and Free Christian Churches in Britain. It has since been used by Unitarian churches in other parts of the world.

Unitarianism values insights from the present as well as the past. It is appropriate therefore that the flaming chalice symbol should have both ancient and modern roots, in both instances grounded in the principles of sacrifice and service to humanity.

Three elements

The symbol of the chalice flame may be further understood as a metaphor for the lives of human beings, both as individuals and in community.

A cup is a familiar object made to be held and passed around – for sharing. A flame, by contrast, is not an object. It cannot be weighed or measured. It is no static thing, but a dynamic, changing process.

The flame needs three elements. The first of these is fuel. Fuel is material – like the human body, like the treasured buildings and books, money and documents of a church community. If a fire lacks fuel it is said to be "burning low" like a candle in its final moments. The flame shrinks until it is just a feeble glow.

Unitarians are not ascetic or "other-worldly" but try to take a realistic and rational view of life. Unitarians readily accept that, like kindling for a fire, people in their private lives and collectively need the fuel of physical things.

The second element is heat. Think of the heat of life itself, distinguishing the living from the dead; the spark of intelligence, the warmth of human encounter, even the friction of disagreement. If a fire lacks heat, as when you dampen a flame with water, it is said to be guttering.

To develop as human beings, people also need heat. The vitality of congregational life, activities which animate and engross, thought-provoking moments that challenge are signs of a healthy liberal religious community. Unitarians believe that society is sustained by the warmth that functioning and supportive communities can provide.

The third element is air. Spirit has always been compared with air, or wind – by Greeks and Hebrews alike. If a fire lacks air, we say that it is smouldering. There is much heat and thick black smoke, but little or no light. Modern life is too often like this.

Unitarians are open to the importance of personal religious experience, whether in chapel on a Sunday, on a mountain-top, or in everyday moments during the working week. To develop, people need air – or spirit: the inspiration, or breathing in, of that invisible, yet vital element; the deep moments of the self in prayer or meditation; the shared movement of the heart when the spirit is felt.

A living flame

Unitarians, unlike Moses, do not simply find the fire burning in the wilderness. The flaming chalice is no burning bush, but something to be lit, and re-lit, by every person. It requires an act of will, of purpose and of faith.

Unitarianism allows persons to develop freely, without the constrictions of received dogma, while experiencing the warmth of community. Unitarians are open to the truths that science has bequeathed, including the truth that darkness has no existence in itself. Darkness is the absence of light. Unitarians believe the way to overcome the darkness is to light our lamps whenever we meet.[3]

What is Unitarianism?

Our Unitarian vision is to provide free and enquiring religion
through the worship of God, the celebration of life, the service of
humanity, and respect for all creation. Unitarians will be a leading
voice and example of liberal faith in Britain; providing welcoming
and growing centres of inspiring worship and inclusive community,
enriched by world faith traditions; committing ourselves to
prophetic witness and social justice.

General Assembly Council vision statement, adopted 1993 [4]

If God is One, we are one with God and with one another in the
universe. For me, these are the true and logical meanings of the
words Unitarian and Universalist.

Yvonne Seon [5]

In this world there have always been many opinions about faith
and salvation. You need not think alike to love alike. There must be
knowledge in faith also. Sanctified reason is the lantern of faith.

Religious reform can never be all at once, but gradually, step by
step. If they offer something better, I will gladly learn. The most
important spiritual function is conscience, the source of all
spiritual joy and happiness. Conscience will not be quieted by
anything less than truth and justice.

We must accept God's truth in this lifetime. Salvation must be
accomplished here on Earth. God is indivisible. *Egy Az Isten.* God
is one.

Francis David (adapted by Richard Fewkes) [6]

This is the mission of our faith: to teach the fragile art of hospitality; to revere both the critical mind and the generous heart; to prove that diversity need not mean divisiveness; and to witness to all that we must hold the whole world in our hands.

William F. Schulz [7]

Love is the doctrine of this church, the quest for truth is its sacrament, and service is its prayer. To dwell together in peace, to seek knowledge in freedom, to serve human need, to the end that all souls shall grow in harmony with the Divine. Thus do we covenant with each other and with God.

Arranged by L. Griswold Williams [8]

Our congregations freely gather to live out a democratic faith.

Every human being is holy and is called to the tasks and joys of love.

We do not limit the truth of God (even to the word "God"), but live in openness and belief in human freedom and dignity.

Our creed is kindness.

We celebrate the gift of life, and join in taking on the sufferings of this fragile world.

We are this generation's bearers of an eternal message, drawn from ancient springs, that truth must grow, enlarge, and glow in creative freedom.

Revelation is not sealed. It is lived anew in every heart.

You say you want it simpler? We join in celebrating one world, one people, one love, which is Truth.

Stephen Kendrick [9]

When asked to define my Unitarianism I usually answer that I believe each life experience is unique, therefore each person's understanding of the spiritual dimension has to be unique, and ultimately we must be our own authority in matters of belief.

Each of us is born with a unique genetic make-up that influences the development of our individual personality. Yet, we do have free will, and our life experiences, our spiritual experiences, our relationship with others, where we are in time and history – all these shape us.

All persons, through their human nature, potentially share the deepest meanings of existence. All of us have the capacity for discovering or responding to "saving truth". Some of our deep experiences shape our perceptions of justice, equality and freedom. These personal experiences may become a driving force – awakening our compassion and leading to social action. We are all responsible for determining and putting into action the right means for a just and peaceful society. We can transcend our situation and we can even change ourselves.

Our individual freedom can only be exercised in the context of relationships with others. In the words of James Luther Adams: "in relationships with others our human nature develops...it is here that our sensibilities about justice, beauty, hope, or meaning are nurtured or stunted... it is here that personal and social freedom lives or dies."

Levels of justice and equity in society determine, in large measure, which aspects of human nature receive fuller expression. As Unitarians we affirm and promote the inherent worth and dignity of every person, and we are inspired to direct our efforts toward the establishment of a just and loving community, in which everyone has an equal chance to fulfil their human potential.

We are dependent for being and for freedom upon a creative power and upon processes not ultimately of our own making. Our creative freedom is the manifestation of this divine and renewing power. Through the use of our creative freedom, we express the highest form of vitality that human existence permits.

Ingrid Tavkar [10]

Dear Friends, stand by this faith. Work for it and sacrifice for it. There is nothing in all the world so important to you as to be loyal to this faith, which has placed before you the loftiest ideals, which has comforted you in sorrow, strengthened you for the noble duty, and made the world beautiful for you. Do not demand immediate results, but rejoice that you are worthy to be entrusted with this great message: that you are strong enough to work for a great true principle without counting the cost. Go on finding ever new applications of these truths and new enjoyments in their contemplation, always trusting in the one God, which ever lives and loves.

Olympia Brown [11]

Unitarians are people who wish their religion to be broad, generously inclusive, and tolerant rather than narrow and dogmatic.

They have a hunger for more freedom, more justice, more fairness, more fulfillment for more of earth's creatures. "Reverence for Life" points us in the right direction: respect for the wonder of creation, which is the root of worship; service whose aim is to enable whatever life we can influence to attain its highest development.

Frank Walker [12]

Be ours a religion which, like sunshine, goes everywhere; its temple, all space; its shrine, the good heart; its creed, all truth; its ritual, works of love; its profession of faith, divine living.

Theodore Parker [13]

I am a Unitarian because this church is the only place where I am both intellectually and spiritually stretched. It is a wonderful fellowship in diversity where doubts and faith, dreams and pragmatism blend together in an utterly satisfying whole. It is somewhere to share ideas and inspirations, celebrations and crises, when I can truly be myself.

Anonymous [14]

Unitarianism is not so much an organized system of religious belief as a religious movement. It is more a method of thought than an outcome. Not that the outcome of Unitarian thought is unimportant. On the contrary, the main beliefs described by that name are of wide philosophical import, and moral necessity to man, which assure their permanent abiding-place among the world's treasures of thought...

The inevitable conclusion... is that this ideal church must rest on the broadest possible basis of fellowship, welcoming to its communion all thoughtful, truth-seeking minds: that any basis of fellowship founded on belief, no matter how wide or rational, is a logical inconsistency in an organization that recognizes the necessity of religious change and progress and makes character, not creed, the test of the religious life.

Celia Parker Woolley [15]

Freedom

It is not surprising that European Unitarians, as oppressed minorities whether in Poland, Transylvania, or the British Isles, should have made this commitment to freedom and tolerance; moreover, this commitment has continued once that oppression has ceased, as it has since 1813 in England and sporadically and briefly in Transylvania... While this commitment originally was motivated by a corporate desire to be free from external oppression, it gradually has been internalized over the years to provide increasing individual freedom and tolerance within the Unitarian movement itself.

Charles A. Howe [16]

We sometimes hear it said by some of our own members that you can believe whatever you please. Actually we are confronted with a paradox; we are not free to believe what we please, we are free to believe what we must!

Burdette Backus [17]

The freedom of the mind is the beginning of all other freedoms.

Clinton Lee Scott [18]

The old watchwords of liberalism – freedom, reason and tolerance – worthy though they be, are simply not catching the imagination of the contemporary world. They describe a process for approaching the religious depths, but they testify to no intimate acquaintance with the depths themselves. If we are ever to speak to a new age, we must supplement our seeking with some profound religious findings.

O. Eugene Pickett [19]

The leading principles of Unitarian Universalism – freedom, reason and tolerance – are instrumental values rather than terminal ones. They are effective vehicles for engaging life's depths and enabling us to create transformative communities of hope and love...

Freedom furnishes the means to pursue our bedrock human purpose: the building of the redemptive community where freethinking mystics with hands can flourish. But freedom *per se* doesn't necessarily get us there. It often takes us on wild goose chases or lures us into blind alleys. Freedom is the condition, not the substance, of truth. Being responsibly free is our objective.

Tom Owen-Towle [20]

The religion that says freedom! – freedom from ignorance and false belief; freedom from spurious claims and bitter prejudices; freedom to seek the truth, both old and new, and freedom to follow it; freedom from the hates and greeds that divide humankind and spill the blood of every generation; freedom for honest thought, freedom for equal justice, freedom to seek the true, the good and the beautiful with minds unimpaired by cramping dogmas and spirits uncrippled by dependence. The religion that says humankind is not divided – except by ignorance and prejudice and hate; the religion that sees humankind as naturally one and waiting to be spiritually united; the religion that proclaims an end to all exclusions – and declares a brother- and sisterhood unbounded! The religion that knows that we shall never find the fullness of the wonder and the glory of life until we are ready to share it, that we shall never have hearts big enough for the love of God until we have made them big enough for the worldwide love of one another.

As you have listened to me, have you thought perchance that this is your religion? If you have, do not congratulate yourself. Stop long enough to recollect the miseries of the world you live in: the fearful cruelties, the enmities, the hate, the bitter prejudices, the need of such a world for such a faith. And if you still can say that this of which I have spoken is your religion, then ask yourself this question: What are you doing with it?

A. Powell Davies [21]

We have before us but the one work to do, that of giving to every human being the fullest possible liberty to develop his or her spirit just in accordance with its own promptings.

Susan B. Anthony [22]

Reason, thinking, and truth-seeking

Over time the traditional Unitarian emphasis on the exercise of
human reason caused Unitarians to cease to regard the Bible as the
ultimate authority in matters of faith; during the 19th century in
particular, it was becoming clear that the Scriptures could justly be
subjected to textual criticism like other works of literature, while
advances in scientific knowledge suggested a different view of the
world and humanity from that presented in the Bible. Thus among
Unitarians of today honest reflection on fundamental religious
questions, illuminated by the insights gained from personal
experience, the Judaeo-Christian tradition, other faiths, science,
psychology, poetry and literature, tends to be seen as providing the
most credible approach to the personal spiritual quest.

Matthew Smith [23]

Should free inquiry lead to the destruction of Christianity itself, it
ought not on that account to be discontinued: for we can only wish
for the prevalence of Christianity on the supposition of its being
true. If we Dissenters be not friends to free enquiry in its utmost
extent, and if we do not give the most unbounded scope to reason
in matters of religion, we shall be absolutely inexcusable.

Joseph Priestley [24]

Only through the revival of ethical and religious thinking can the
spirit arise which will give to mankind the knowledge and the
strength to lead it out of darkness and conflict to light and peace.
Liberal Christianity has the great responsibility of bringing to men
and maintaining in them the conviction that thought and religion are
not incompatible, but belong together. All deep religious thinking
becomes thoughtful; all truly profound thinking becomes religious.

Albert Schweitzer [25]

I call that mind free which masters the senses, and which recognizes its own reality and greatness: which passes life, not in asking what it shall eat or drink, but in hungering, thirsting, and seeking after righteousness.

I call that mind free which jealously guards its intellectual rights and powers, which does not content itself with a passive or hereditary faith: which opens itself to light whencesoever it may come; which receives new truth as an angel from heaven.

I call that mind free which is not passively framed by outward circumstances, and is not the creature of accidental impulse: which discovers everywhere the radiant signatures of the infinite spirit, and in them finds help to its own spiritual enlargement.

I call that mind free which protects itself against the usurpations of society, and which does not cower to human opinion: which refuses to be the slave or tool of the many or of the few, and guards its empire over itself as nobler than the empire of the world.

I call that mind free which resists the bondage of habit, which does not mechanically copy the past, nor live on its old virtues: but listens for new and higher notions of conscience, and rejoices to pour itself forth in fresh and higher exertions.

I call that mind free which sets no bounds to its love, which, wherever they are seen, delights in virtue and sympathizes with suffering: which recognizes in all human beings the image of God and the rights of God's children, and offers itself up a willing sacrifice to the cause of humankind.

I call that mind free which has cast off all fear but that of wrongdoing, and which no menace or peril can enthrall: which is calm in the midst of tumults, and possesses itself, though all else will be lost.

William Ellery Channing [26]

Faith which refuses to face indisputable facts is but little faith. Truth is always gain, however hard it is to accommodate ourselves to it. To linger in any kind of untruth proves to be a departure from the straight way of faith.

Albert Schweitzer [27]

An unexamined faith is not worth having, for it can only be true by accident. A faith worth having is a faith worth discussing and testing. To believe that a fence of taboo should be built around some formulation is to believe that a person can become God (or his exclusive private secretary) and speak for him. No authority, including the authority of individual conviction, is rightly exempt from discussion and criticism. The faith of the free, if it is to escape the tyranny of the arbitrary, must be available to all, testable by all (and not merely by an elite), valid for all. It is something that is intelligible and justifiable.

James Luther Adams [28]

Let's not think so much that we forget to feel.

Roger Cowan [29]

The ideal in religion is to establish the proper balance between mind and emotion.

Waldemar Argow [30]

In one sermon he [Francis David] wrote: "Let reflection be spontaneous." In this instance the word "spontaneous" means natural, according to the laws of nature. "Spontaneous reflection," he said, "is like a bird on the wing, and one can neither raise mountains nor any other impediments [to stop it]..." He continued, "In the way of reason – a God-given light – you cannot build walls; light penetrates above them... God's word needs neither to be forced upon faith nor stopped like a stone, but wants rather to flow like water."

Imre Gellérd [31]

As a liberal traditionalist, I am also an existentialist, a relativist and a pragmatist. By existentialist I mean that truth must take its origin and be confirmed in personal experience. By relativist I see truth and human understanding of truth as inextricably related, so that the strongest truth claims must be made in a spirit of humility. And by pragmatist I look for the meaning of language in the live effects of ideas named, not in dictionaries.

Alice Blair Wesley [32]

I feel an increased sense of urgency to explore my thoughts – not because I'm afraid I might die tomorrow unsaved, but because I want to live tomorrow a bit more informed and centered.

Hafidha Acuay [33]

Tolerance

The understanding and practice of toleration among Unitarians has been historically progressive. Three stages of this progression are observable.

First of all, toleration starts when brave individuals, like David Ferenc [Francis David] in Transylvania, assert their rights of private judgement over creeds, confessions of faith and autocratic church authorities, and then demand not just their right to think differently, but also that the church authority tolerates their difference.

Secondly, the growth of toleration then moves, as it did in England and Wales, Scotland and Ireland, to the toleration of organised religious "oppositions" to the state churches. The new legal religious toleration then expands to include political toleration as well.

Thirdly, the final stage of religious toleration is achieved when members of a community, religious or otherwise, don't just tolerate (which still has an element of judgement about it) but actually accept those who are different culturally, politically or religiously alongside them. Many Unitarian communities – especially in the English-speaking world – have arrived at this stage within their congregations.

The common factor is being human, and our comprehension of the larger view is humanly limited. "My view is incomplete, therefore my neighbour's view is incomplete but maybe together our views may be a little more complete than they are apart."

That is why Unitarians have moved from seeking toleration for their own differences to seeking toleration for the differences of others; and why Unitarians have moved beyond generous and non-critical acceptance of the differences of others to critical and open sharing of their mutual differences.

Andrew Hill [34]

It was only when I was invited to join an adult RE course, called *Building Your Own Theology,* that I realised how truly tolerant Unitarians are. Week after week I listened, enthralled, as we all grappled with our beliefs, our uncertainties – the questions that our lives had forced us to consider. I met a minister who wasn't sure if God existed; I met people whose faith had been strengthened by adversity, and those for whom firm beliefs were no longer of value. I learnt that Unitarians, by and large, are spiritual folk who can stand the terror of uncertainty – who can accept that, in matters religious, "We just don't know for sure."

By sitting together in religious education groups, Unitarians are doing far more than just "tolerating" each other. By truly listening to one another – by creating spaces where we can share one another's stories, hopes and fears – we affirm the right of individuals to express themselves fully and to be heard and accepted for who they are, unique human beings.

Sarah Tinker [35]

Tolerance is not an end in itself but a means towards the development of Truth and community. One implication of this is that there are situations where tolerance is not the best attitude.

Earl Morse Wilbur (historian of Unitarianism) observed that tolerance was one enduring characteristic (with freedom and reason) of Unitarianism. But converting this observation into a defining principle sells us, our religion, and our movement short.

It is helpful to think of tolerance in the context of the values of Truth, Love, and Beauty that it serves. These values shape the religious quest, guiding and motivating but never fully realised. Tolerance, while also a means towards community and aesthetics, is most clearly part of the Truth-struggle. One reason for its emphasis in Unitarian thinking is our focus on trying to discover, and lead our lives in harmony with, the Truth. In our battles with creeds that attempt to confine the Truth, we can easily forget that the Love-struggle and the Beauty-struggle are just as important in developing our human/divine potential.

There may be times when we cannot be true to higher values and tolerate something. This is perhaps clearest in relation to Love, for when we love someone we cannot tolerate their exploitation. The more deeply and widely we love, the less we can tolerate exploitation, whether we are talking about racial hatred or child abuse. It is good to be tolerant, but it is better and more purposeful to be loving.

John Clifford [36]

Tolerance and Freedom... are still much needed in our conflict-ridden world, but they need to be expanded beyond the anthropocentric context of the Enlightenment, to embrace a deep reverence for the ecology of all creation. For humans to be more tolerable on this planet, we must be less tolerant of abuse of the world and its natural resources – perpetrated by ourselves and our fellow humans (particularly first-world Westerners). Our freedoms must be circumscribed, by the limits of sustainability and the principles of nature... For those of us, like myself, grown greedy for more than our fair share of the earth's resources, we have much to give up.

Peter Hawkins [37]

Unity and diversity

It is possible that the twenty-first century may see the emergence of a commitment to pluralism as a *fourth* defining Unitarian principle, one emerging out of the internalized commitments to freedom and tolerance. Certainly the makeup of the International Council of Unitarians and Universalists suggests this, as does the roster of Unitarian groups presently existing in Europe. While tradition and the cultural climate in Romania may keep the Transylvanian Unitarians united in theology and practice, it is evident from the 1990 statement of the Objects Review Commission of the General Assembly that British Unitarianism is moving towards a pluralistic self-image not unlike that which American Unitarian Universalists have recently embraced. The most important question facing Unitarians in the next century may well be whether a pluralistic religious movement can survive and prosper.

Charles A. Howe [38]

I think that one of our most important tasks is to convince others that there's nothing to fear in difference; that difference, in fact, is one of the healthiest and most invigorating of human characteristics, without which life would become meaningless. Here the lies the power of the liberal way: not in making the whole world Unitarian, but in helping ourselves and others to see some of the possibilities inherent in viewpoints other than one's own; in encouraging the free interchange of ideas; in welcoming fresh approaches to the problems of life; in urging the fullest, most vigorous use of critical self-examination.

Adlai Stevenson [39]

What unites us is not what we say but what we seek, not a common avowal of faith but a common purpose.

Anonymous [40]

Allow your ministers the liberty that ye take for yourselves, and take no umbrage if, in consequence of giving more attention to matters of theology than you have leisure for, they should entertain opinions different from yours... it is no great hardship upon you to give them at least a dispassionate and attentive hearing. They cannot force any opinions upon you. You still have the power of judging for yourselves; and without hearing you cannot have even the means of forming a right judgment. And where an agreement cannot be had (and few persons who really think for themselves will agree in all things), you may exercise that mutual candour, which is of more value than any agreement in speculation.

Joseph Priestley [41]

Harmony exists in difference no less than in likeness.

Margaret Fuller [42]

A key unifying factor in our variously named member congregations is that we do not require any formal statement of belief for ministry or membership. We take pride in being a creedless religious community, but we do this because we value individual religious expression and commitment too highly to allow coercion by others. Our aversion to creeds, however, should not be allowed to become an aversion to content. Each of us should have a developing religious perspective whose content we can share with others. Our promotion of the richness of diversity will appear very shallow to outsiders if all we offer is a content-free process.

John Clifford [43]

Community and covenant

Community and autonomy do not exclude one another, but enhance one another, for the essential function of the congregation is to link the individual to a religious community. It is to mediate between the individual and the "church universal". It is to link the local congregation with other congregations and indeed with peoples of faith universally.

The Commission on Appraisal of the Unitarian Universalist Association [44]

If, recognizing the interdependence of all life, we strive to build community, the strength we gather will be our salvation. If you are black and I am white, it will not matter. If you are female and I am male, it will not matter. If you are older and I am younger, it will not matter. If you are progressive and I am conservative, it will not matter. If you are straight and I am gay, it will not matter. If you are Christian and I am Jewish, it will not matter.

If we join spirits as brothers and sisters, the pain of our aloneness will be lessened, and that does matter. In this spirit, we build community and move toward restoration.

Marjorie Bowens-Wheatley [45]

As a religious heritage bonded not by a creed, confession, or common prayer but by covenant, Unitarian Universalists vow to stay at the table long enough to understand one another and mold a viable community. Ours is a fellowship united not by law but by loyalty, by faithfulness of vows rather than sameness of beliefs. We promise to hold and be held by one another. We pledge our troth or trust. Fidelity, internal discipline, and mutual responsibility are required in a covenantal faith in order to work out our differences together.

Tom Owen-Towle [46]

Humanistic liberalism constantly aims to promote the widest possible human comradeship and the closest possible human fellowship. And this aim is underwritten by the knowledge that co-operation and not competition is the dominant factor in the growth of the race.

Curtis W. Reese [47]

For me, the essentials of Unitarianism are summarised in the words of Jesus in the Gospel of Thomas that sounds something like "The Kingdom of God is within you and all around you." The Kingdom of God – the divine, the Truth – is within me. I do not need anyone to mediate between me and the ultimate Truth. I, as an individual, have access to the most important religious Truth. No one can tell me what to believe, no one can claim to know better, religious authority is with me, the individual. And yet, the Truth is not just within me, it is also all around me, it is in all other people as well, just as much as it is in me, and maybe some truth can only be revealed in relationship and through dialogue. That is why we need community. As a Unitarian I have an obligation to listen to my inner self, the voice of God within me, and also to listen to the voice of God in all other people. I have to listen to the voice of God speaking in other people in my congregation as well as all people I come across in my life. I am an individual-in-community, and it is only by respecting both poles of individuality and community that I can form a genuine truth-seeking, life-giving faith.

Stephen Lingwood [48]

If you want to make changes in people's lives, in their worlds, then it's going to happen in the church. By the way, at the beginning of our [Unitarian Universalist] Principles, it states: "We covenant to affirm and promote..." Covenant is the commitment we make to each other in religious community – not as isolated individuals, but in community. We enter the covenant as individuals, but in covenant we agree to be and work together. In other words, the Principles are to be lived out and worked for in church, with church.

Fredric John Muir [49]

Love

"You shall love the Lord your God with all your heart, and with all your soul, and with all your mind." This is the greatest and first commandment. And a second is like it: "You shall love your neighbour as yourself." On these two commandments hang all the law and the prophets.

Jesus of Nazareth [50]

The spirit of Love will be intensified to Godly proportions when reciprocal love exists between the entire human race and each of its individual members. That love must be based upon mutual respect for the differences in color, language, and worship, even as we appreciate and accept with gratitude the differences that tend to unite the male and female of all species. We do not find those differences obstacles to love.

George de Benneville [51]

I believe that there are four interlocking and overlapping loves in life that must be equally and constantly cultivated: love of self, neighbor, the natural world, and divine mystery. Corollaries: (1) Love exists only in action; and (2) loving up-close furnishes life's most rugged chore.

Tom Owen-Towle [52]

We need – need terribly – a new liberation of the human spirit. We need love again: not the little thing the foolish modern songs are sung about, the paltry caricature that has been held up to our young people and the leaden counterfeit with which our older people have tried to content themselves. We need love as the apostle Paul spoke of it: the love without which no merit could avail and no virtue endure; the love that "beareth all things, believeth all things, hopeth all things, endureth all things"; the love "that never faileth".

A. Powell Davies [53]

My personal creed, essentially Universalism of the old school with modern vocabulary and philosophical foundations, is as follows: God is Love and we are creatures of Love. We are created, nurtured, and fulfilled by creative love working within us, through us, and amongst us, creating Truth and Beauty, Healing and Wholeness. Value arises from the activity of God's creative, dynamic Spirit, and value-oriented communities are central to developing individual potential and enabling just communities. Religion is more a matter of spiritual awareness and practical commitment than it is of rational theology...

Universalist theology starts with a God of Love, but it very quickly moves to an awareness of the reality and universality of suffering and builds its sense of ministry to the world on these twin foundations.

John Clifford [54]

Jesus was sure that harmony with God can only be obtained through perfect love, and that such love can never be free from pain, for it is never free from effort and failure; and the way of perfect love is the way of the cross.

Gertrude von Petzold [55]

Freedom, reason, tolerance and pluralism aren't enough, not on their own. We need a message to give to people, Good News to preach. What Good News can Unitarians give to the world? Just this: love. A Holy Love that transforms, that is powerful and prophetic and justice-seeking. This message has always been at the heart of our faith: from Francis David, who said "you need not think alike to love alike", to the Universalists who knew that nothing will ever separate anyone from the love of God, even to today when Unitarians work to support the rights of gay couples because we know that love is always a blessing, regardless of gender.

Stephen Lingwood [56]

Love, Hope, Reverence are realities of a different order from the senses, but they are positive and constant facts, always active, always working out mighty changes in human life.

Elizabeth Blackwell [57]

Open, inclusive, and welcoming churches

My understanding of myself as a minister begins to emerge as, in faith, I begin to focus my life more upon my liberation than upon my oppression, seeking the places where I can include instead of focusing on the places where I am excluded. In the past few years, I have found tremendous meaning and sustaining power in my relationships with people whom the church and society have consistently devalued: incarcerated women, persons with AIDS and mental disabilities, lesbians, and gay men. It is in these relationships that I have begun to see the Spirit shaping a ministry of mutuality – a ministry with, rather than a ministry to, which so easily becomes a ministry at. In the poorest quadrant of Washington, DC, we provide nurture and challenge to any willing to affirm a simple covenant of love. Together, we seek and find joy in relationship and glory in struggle.

Alma Faith Crawford [58]

We would be wrong to assume that people investigate our churches solely, or even primarily because they might find a particular service interesting. For many, the search is for community as much as for intellectual enlightenment, and any Unitarian group must present itself to newcomers as a caring, friendly, non-threatening gathering, in which Freedom, Reason, and Tolerance are part of the fabric and not just part of the rhetoric. Visitors must be put at their ease, and the role of the "welcomer" is a very important one in this regard, involving more than just handing out hymnbooks. Coffee-time after the service also provides a unique and vital opportunity to make visitors feel welcome and valued and, while they should never be subject to lengthy monologues by garrulous or proselytising members of the congregation, visitors should never have to stand alone at this time, and should be given every opportunity to introduce themselves.

Bill Darlison [59]

We live in a world where people are damned in the name of religion because their views are different, are verbally and physically attacked because either the hue of their skin or the manner of their loving is different. Those of us who are held fast in the grasp of a loving faith must demonstrate an alternative way of being – the Universalist way of unqualified acceptance.

Tom Owen-Towle [60]

Dialogue

Let love continue. If we agree in love, there is no disagreement that can do us any injury; but if we do not, no other agreement can do us any good. Let us keep a secret guard against the enemy that sows discord among us. Let us endeavor to keep the unity of spirit in the bonds of peace.

Hosea Ballou [61]

A dialogue by members of the world community which promotes peace requires risk. The risk includes the possibility of arousing anger and hostility in the expression of strongly held conflicting views. Perhaps an even greater risk is the surprise in receiving new insights that require changing your own perspective. It is possible that you could discover unexplored horizons of meaning and truth. In real engagement with another person, you cannot fully foresee what will happen. At the same time, risk must be matched by trust. To expose yourself to the analysis and challenge of another person requires trust. Dialogue depends on trust that the other person is also caring, is secure enough in his or her view to allow for differences, and is open to learning new dimensions of his or her orientation that may be evoked in dialogue.

Frederick J. Streng [62]

Nothing is ever said until someone listens.

Paul Carnes [63]

So often Unitarian discourse can become serial monologues or debate. Now debate is similar to discussion, a word which comes from the same root as "percussion" and "concussion" and is about hitting the other person with your pre-formed ideas, while they hit you with theirs. Negotiation or mediation is often a modified version of this, which creates a compromise position. Transformational learning has still not happened. In dialogue ("knowing emerging between"), each person endeavours, while remaining true to his or her own experience, to be open or receptive enough to respect the reality of the other, within his or her own field of experience. This creates a flow of knowing between the participants.

Peter Hawkins [64]

I think we need to learn to have radically honest, radically open conversations when we really listen to each other. This should be a fundamental Unitarian spiritual practice. We need to understand each other's life histories, where we come from, where we are going, and how these things shape our viewpoints. We need to be able to empathise with other people, not demonise one another. We need to be able to announce what we believe and how we feel without judgment. Then engage in a truth-seeking conversation. Then we need to sit in silence and remember that there is a place where words end.

Stephen Lingwood [65]

The purpose of church

The central task of the religious community is to unveil the bonds that bind each to all. There is a connectedness, a relationship discovered amid the particulars of our own lives and the lives of others. Once felt, it inspires us to act for justice.

It is the church that assures us that we are not struggling for justice on our own, but as members of a larger community. The religious community is essential, for alone our vision is too narrow to see all that must be seen, and our strength too limited to do all that must be done. Together, our vision widens and our strength is renewed.

Mark Morrison-Reed [66]

Blessed are those who yearn for deepening more than escape; who are not afraid to grow in spirit.

Blessed are those who take seriously the bonds of community, who regularly join in celebration and learning; who come as much to minister as to be ministered unto.

Blessed are those who bring their children; who invite their friends to come along, to join in fellowship, service, learning, and growth.

Blessed are those who support the church and its work by their regular, sustained and generous giving; and who give of themselves no less than their money.

Blessed are those who know that the church is often imperfect, yet rather than harbor feelings of anger or disappointment, bring their concerns and needs to the attention of the church leaders.

Blessed are those who, when asked to serve, do it gladly; who realize that change is brought about through human meeting, who do the work of committees, and stay till the end.

Blessed are those who speak their minds in meetings, who can take and give criticism; who keep alive their sense of humor.

Blessed are those who know that the work of the church is the transformation of society; who have a vision of Beloved Community transcending the present, and who do not shrink from controversy, sacrifice, or change.

Blessed are they indeed.

John Buehrens [67]

If we do not need a mediator between ourselves and the divine, we can worship anywhere. Daily living can be infused with spirituality. Private meditation and prayer are possible in any space, and that space – home, office, garden – can be made sacred by those acts of prayer or meditation. Reflection on things that are of timeless importance to us can – and often does – take place in our own armchairs. Our own life experiences form the basis of our religious education. In these circumstances, gathering together in a religious association may appear to be not only unnecessary, but even potentially damaging to the individual life of the spirit.

This last statement needs elaboration. Why should we fear meeting with others to share our religious views? First of all, because it requires time and effort. Both these things are in short supply in many people's lives, where so many things jostle for attention. Second, it requires commitment. It requires the acceptance of common points of agreement to enable an individual to declare that his or her views belong in a particular category. It is one thing to be able to say that, from all one has learned and read and observed, one is a Unitarian. It is quite another to allow the name *Unitarian* to become a public identifier of one's nature – to wear the label, with all that this implies. Third, it requires courage: the courage to meet strangers, and open our deep thoughts to them; the courage to debate religious matters, about which we may feel very strongly, with those who may differ from us; and the courage to be open to the possibility of change and growth. Just when we thought we had our world-view worked out to our own satisfaction, along comes someone with a different perspective which we cannot ignore...

The challenge for today's religious organizations, then, is to meet the religious needs of individuals without imposing a ready-made religion upon them. It would seem, at least in principle, that this is what Unitarianism is best able to do.

Kay Millard [68]

The world is full of beauty: we need to express our wonder, praise and thankfulness, our gratitude for the privilege of life.

The world is full of suffering, tragedy and horror: we need courage and strength to face them.

These are both good reasons for cherishing a religious home – a church.

People need a community where they can find reverence, beauty, meaning in life, the warmth of mutual support and sympathy, and the will to reach out in service to the world.

You may share this view yourself.

You may believe that the spiritual life is a reality – the life of appreciation and devoted care that reaches out in generous self-giving. Nevertheless, you cannot believe the dogmas that churches expect you to believe before they will fully accept you.

If this is your outlook, you may find that the... Unitarian Church can offer you a home. The Unitarian Church is not exclusive: it welcomes all seekers after truth...

Most churches find their bond of union in scriptural or creedal affirmations. All who wish to be members are expected to profess exactly the same theological beliefs, and undergo the same rituals.

The Unitarian bond of union is different. Unitarians believe that people can covenant to work together for the deepening of spiritual life, the strengthening of moral character, and the improvement of society without conforming to a set pattern of theological dogmas. Unitarians hold that differing theological views are natural and healthy, and that attempts to enforce conformity are deadening and potentially destructive. History is witness to the horrors of religious intolerance.

Unitarians wish their church to help them face together life's spiritual challenges. The church helps people to come to their own individual conclusions and forge their own personal faith.

Frank Walker [69]

Why belong to any church at all? Can't I be a "Unitarian" without belonging? Not really. Most of us aren't resolute or gifted enough to achieve our full potential living as hermits. Good company helps.

Anonymous [70]

Do we go to church in order to look into the darkness of our souls and face the hard truths of our existence? Do we go to church to gain the courage and community we need in order to make the courageous leap of faith into the terrifying truths of our lives? Do we go to church to stand over-against ourselves and pull ourselves into the hard truths of our existence?

Thandeka [71]

In the First Unitarian Church of Chicago we started a program of "aggressive love" to try to [racially] desegregate that Gothic cathedral. We had two members of the Board objecting. Unitarianism had no creed, they said, and we were making desegregation into a creed. It was a gentle but firm disagreement, and a couple of us kept pressing. "Well, what do you say is the purpose of this church?" we asked, and we kept it up until about 1:30 in the morning. We were all worn out, when finally this man made one of the great statements, for my money, in the history of religion. "O.K., Jim. The purpose of this church ... well, the purpose of this church is to get hold of people like me and change them."

James Luther Adams [72]

The prophethood of all believers

Our tradition has articulated and emphasized the notion, not only of the *priesthood* of all believers, but also of the *prophethood* of all believers. This means especially the capacity and the right to participate in the shaping of the congregation. This prophethood belongs not merely to the clergy: it belongs to the congregation and to the individuals in the congregation. But authentic prophecy does not appear very often within the churches; therefore it had to appear in nonreligious, or even antichurch communities.

James Luther Adams [73]

Always it is easier to pay homage to prophets than to heed the direction of their vision. It is easier blindly to venerate the saints than to learn the human quality of their sainthood. It is easier to glorify the heroes of the race than to give weight to their examples. To worship the wise is much easier than to profit by their wisdom.

Great leaders are honored, not by adulation, but by sharing their insights and values. Grandchildren of those who stoned the prophet sometimes gather up the stones to build the prophet's monument. Always it is easier to pay homage to prophets than to heed the direction of their vision.

Clinton Lee Scott [74]

We are a liberal church community which has not only dared to preach freedom but to live freedom as well, which has not only prophesied a more just day to come but has dared to live prophetically right now.

Mark Belletini [75]

Keepers of the dream will come again and again, from what humble places we do not know, to struggle against the crushing odds, leaving behind no worldly kingdom, but only a gleam in the dark hills to show how high we may climb. Already there have been many such heroes – women and men whose names we do not know, but whose words and deeds still light the path for us.

H. G. Wenzel [76]

Worship

Worship should be a *revelation*, not of God's message delivered finally twenty centuries ago but of his presence and inspiration in all ages and times, especially here and now through his children and to each of them, even the humblest.

Aurelia Henry Reinhardt [77]

The bond of unity in a church is not a shared belief but a shared worship. Worship (worth-ship) is an act of reverence for what is regarded as of great, or supreme, worth. In the ultimate analysis this is but another way of capturing the true meaning of love. What is of real worth to us, in the full sense, we cannot help but love. Love is reverence for life, to use Albert Schweitzer's phrase, and reverence is a mode of worship. Worship in a Unitarian setting becomes a shared act of celebration, expressing our love for things of worth – those values by which and for which we live, in whatever picture-language they may be symbolized.

Phillip Hewett [78]

To worship is to stand in awe under a heaven of stars, before a flower, a leaf in sunlight, or a grain of sand. To worship is to be silent, receptive, before a tree astir with the wind, or the passing shadow of a cloud. To worship is to work with dedication and with skill, it is to pause from work and listen to a strain of music. To worship is to sing with the singing beauty of the earth; it is to listen through the storm to the still, small voice within. Worship is loneliness seeking communion; it is a thirsty land crying out for rain. Worship is kindred fire within our hearts; it moves through deeds of kindness and through acts of love. Worship is the mystery within us reaching out to the mystery beyond. It is an inarticulate silence yearning to speak; it is the window of the moment open to the sky of the eternal.

Jacob Trapp [79]

It would certainly be found desirable that the people should themselves have a large share in the performance of the service, as the intermixture of their voices would both introduce more variety and greater animation... The deep silence of listening expectation, the burst of united praises, the solemn pauses that invite reflection... would swell and melt the heart by turns.

Anna Laetitia Aikin Barbauld [80]

We are gradually and more or less painfully learning that spirituality is not primarily a question of listening to uplifting words from the pulpit, although they can open windows for a brief glimpse into a more complex terrain of experience. Nor is spiritual development guaranteed by withdrawal from everyday life into meditation and stillness, in order to disengage from the preoccupations of our selfish egos.

Despite being a time-honoured path, and an element of the collective practice of many religious communities, meditation is not sufficient in itself. Some Unitarians feel that the period of silent meditation during the Sunday service is the most important part of worship. (Incidentally, this and the singing are the only truly egalitarian moments in our traditional worship services.) I believe that it fits Unitarian self-understanding better to focus on what many modern spiritual seekers are striving towards: participatory and co-equal forms of spiritual inquiry and celebration. I believe we must question our tendency to delegate responsibility for our holistic development to a "specialist" in matters spiritual.

Michaela von Britzke [81]

Sunday worship is at the heart of what we do. If it has no appeal, visitors will not return. One rule seems to apply: whatever you do, do it well. For example, if singing is not your congregation's strong point, don't insist on five hymns. Practise the hymns that you do sing (with the aid of a competent musician), and help visiting preachers to choose hymns which everyone in the congregation knows or can learn easily. It is much more important that the hymns be sung well than that they perfectly echo the theme of the address...

Above all, the service, however it is constructed, should be a *religious* service, which allows participants to explore and express their deeply felt spiritual needs and longings. Unitarian ministers and worship leaders are not principally political activists, low-paid social workers, or untrained counsellors. A Unitarian congregation is not the religious wing of the Green Party or the Labour Party or the Liberal Democrats. Worship should not be primarily concerned with feminism, unemployment, world hunger, gay liberation, or cleaning up the environment. These are all tangential issues with which individuals and even groups within a congregation should engage... but they should not dominate Sunday worship. People come to church to pray, to praise, to give thanks, to come to terms with their own deepest reckonings; to investigate the ultimate issues about life and death, to ask why they are in pain and what they can do about it. They don't come to church to be told constantly about their political and social responsibilities. They don't come to join a discussion group dominated by an opinionated minority. They don't come to hear religious polemic or sniping at orthodoxy. They don't come to hear about the glories of our Unitarian past. They don't come to hear every word spoken by the preacher scrutinised for political correctness. They don't come for interminable arguments about words. They don't come to be told, week after week, that a Unitarian is free to follow his or her own individual religious path. They come for guidance on that path, and if they don't get it, they will go elsewhere.

Bill Darlison [82]

Religious education

Religious education for children is designed to: Encourage spiritual awakening and development. Build on a child's natural sense of wonder. Channel positively the impulse to enquire and create. Share stories from our religious inheritance and from other faiths.

General Assembly of Unitarian and Free Christian Churches [83]

What is the role of religious education in the Unitarian and Free Christian movement today? Can it make a difference in our wider society? Liberal religious education for me has huge potential. Its essence is not the teaching of "facts", although knowledge is very useful to us. Nor is it the establishment of faith, although faith can be truly sustaining. The essence of liberal religious education has to be an exploration, alone and with others, which allows us to live more fully, more responsibly, more responsively. Remember the dictum, attributed to Margaret Mead and immortalised on a Wayside Pulpit poster many years ago: "*Never doubt that a small group of committed people can change the world. Indeed, they are the only thing that can*". Imagine that a few thousand Unitarians and Free Christians in the early years of the third millennium were able and willing to speak powerfully about their faith and about the value of free enquiry into religious matters. Religious education courses would help people to find their spiritual voices, encourage people to ask searching questions of themselves and one another, and enable people to clarify their values and beliefs, thus building spiritual intelligence as a contribution to the future of our species.

Sarah Tinker [84]

There is no money lost that is used in educating the people.

Olympia Brown [85]

It has been my experience, in visiting primary-school classrooms, that in a context where teachers are concerned to draw out what is in the child, and to lead the child into productive and caring relationships in society, children are genuinely concerned for one another and make room for each other to shine, as well as being delighted in their own learning.

Anne McClelland [86]

Congregational polity

The General Assembly has no control over its constituent congregations and fellowships. There may be shared values, but there is no uniform product or service – no identical offering – that can be delivered nationwide to a centrally agreed master plan. Nor should there be, for that would be contrary to the Unitarian ethos. However, congregational independence and autonomy presents challenges – as well as opportunities – in strengthening the Unitarian witness and widening the circle of community. The General Assembly can encourage, influence, and support – as indeed it does – but what happens at local level depends ultimately on the will of the congregation.

Christine Hayhurst [87]

I am inclined to think that congregational democracy is responsible for a lot of the intransigence in the movement. In the Church of England and Church of Scotland, there are higher authorities (bishops, presbyteries, and so on) who can ensure that congregations conform to the ideals of the denomination, and even close down a church if low membership or inadequate finances make it non-viable. Of course, this goes against Unitarian principles of individualism and self-determination, but, in the interests of survival, has the time not come when we should be thinking that the label "Unitarian" is a franchise, and presupposes a number of recognisable key elements?

George Chryssides [88]

We have called attention to the paradigm shift in liberal religious thought as a whole – from independence to interdependence, from individualism to relationalism. We believe that thinking of congregational polity only as a principle of local autonomy disempowers us. We believe that understanding congregational polity as the principle of "a community of autonomous congregations" empowers us as it is more in keeping with our spiritual vision of who we are and what we seek to become.

The Commission on Appraisal of the Unitarian Universalist Association [89]

Outreach, sharing, and growth

As far as proselytising is concerned, Unitarians in Britain are becoming aware that they are hiding their light under a bushel, and that attempts at publicising the denomination are no bad thing. If there is slight growth in future years, this is likely to come from those who are currently "unchurched", and a few who come to be disenchanted with dogmatism of much mainstream religion.

George Chryssides [90]

Our liberal religious approach has a unique gift to share, and we should be able and willing to share it, but to do this effectively, we each have to search our hearts for the lure, the sense of importance and direction that represents our patterning of our lives in response to a God of Love. This patterning includes action and resource priorities. If our churches do not adequately minister, they will be swept aside by some developing form of community valuing... and will deserve to be swept aside... The answer is not to shift responsibility for our ministry even further onto a dedicated few. The answer is not to expect some other level of organisation to do our ministry for us. The answer is not to crouch in fear of being swept away, rather to commit our individual selves to shared ministry and commit our resources in line with our truly-felt value of our congregations, which we claim to love. Think on it: We are aware of being part of a dynamic creative force whose beauty and complexity stretch from the majesty of the cosmos to the quantum workings of particles we can only see at third hand. And in our fear and partial understandings we pull back from the very commitment that would make us effective ministers to our suffering world and its inhabitants.

John Clifford [91]

Each one of us has a part to play in widening the circle of the Unitarian community, and we must all work together to this end.

Anonymous [92]

Go out into the highways and by-ways... Give the people... something of your new vision. You may possess only a small light but uncover it, let it shine, use it in order to bring more light and understanding to the hearts and minds of men and women. Give them, not Hell, but hope and courage. Do not push them deeper into their theological despair, but teach the kindness and everlasting love of God.

John Murray [93]

Global Unitarianism and Universalism

We, the member groups of the International Council of Unitarians and Universalists, affirming our belief in religious community based on:

- liberty of conscience and individual thought in matters of faith,
- the inherent worth and dignity of every person,
- justice and compassion in human relations,
- responsible stewardship of earth's living system,
- and our commitment to democratic principles,

declare our purposes to be:

- to serve the Infinite Spirit of Life and the human community, by strengthening the worldwide Unitarian and Universalist faith,
- to affirm the variety and richness of our living traditions,
- to facilitate mutual support among member organizations,
- to promote our ideals and principles around the world,
- to provide models of liberal religious response to the human condition which upholds our common values.

Preamble to the constitution of the International Council of Unitarians and Universalists [94]

O God, root and source of body and soul, we ask for boldness in confronting evil. When you are within us, we have the power to counter all that is untrue. O Father and Mother of all humankind, may we redeem our failings by the good work that we do. In the name of the one, the only God.

Prayer from the Unitarian Church of the Khasi Hills of India [95]

[Unitarian] Universalism in the Philippines is a minority theology in the midst of Roman Catholicism. It is a minority faith among the minority. The late Rev. Quimada planted the seed of Universalism and it is growing. But it is "growing in pain". It is up to the present generation of [Unitarian] Universalists to take good care and nourish the growing seed. Being the daughter and a witness to the hard labors of my father in spreading the message of Universalism in the Philippines, I cannot conceive in the remotest corner of my mind that the seed "growing in pain" will die. I cannot imagine that the faith he died so violently defending will be forgotten, unremembered, and neglected in the minds of Unitarians and Universalists in the rest of the world.

Rebecca Quimada Sienes, Philippines [96]

Infinite Spirit of Life, we ask thy blessing on these thy messengers of fellowship and love.

May they remind us, amid diversities of knowledge and of gifts, to be one in desire and affection and devotion to thy holy will.

May they also remind us of the value of comradeship, of doing and sharing alike.

May we cherish friendship as one of thy most precious gifts.

May we not let awareness of another's talents discourage us, or sully our relationship, but may we realize that whatever we can do, great or small, the efforts of all of us are needed to do thy work in this world.

Consecration of the flowers for the Flower Communion by Norbert F. Capek [97]

Where, if anywhere, has persecution and derision of true knowledge and its teachers been greater than among us? Yet this has been the fate of all who have carried the truth ever since the Lord Christ.

George Enyedi [98]

[President Thabo] Mbeki said it was necessary to find a way of co-operating with religious bodies in healing the whole of South African society, black and white, who were all victims of the apartheid era, in a joint effort to recover the damage done by apartheid with which we are all still struggling.

Motivated by the need to engage in our country's issues in this increasingly favourable national climate for liberal religion, we in the Cape Town Unitarian Church see this as an enormous opportunity for outreach and involvement. We intend taking up this challenge with our fellow Unitarians in other parts of the country on a national basis. Who knows, we may well become a national voice, as small as we are! Our size should not limit the quality of our input to the national debate, nor its effect!

Gordon Oliver [99]

Ecumenical and interfaith issues

In 1992, the British Council of Churches (BCC) reorganised itself as a result of the Roman Catholics' willingness to become part of an ecumenical body. The BCC became the Council of Churches for Britain and Ireland (CCBI). Previously the Unitarians had belonged to the BCC as "Associate Members": that is to say, representatives might attend meetings and participate in BCC events, but had no voting rights. When the BCC became the CCBI, Unitarians applied for full membership. They were not accepted, although they were recommended to apply for "observer status". Again they were turned down, although the Society of Friends (the Quakers) were accepted. The Quakers were disappointed with this decision, since Quakers and Unitarians have regarded themselves as having much in common. However, Unitarians will contribute to work with mainstream Christians wherever this is possible, with or without formal acceptance.

George Chryssides [100]

Jesus was, and is, the focus of a dynamic community dedicated to the remaking of humankind. There are other such communities focused on other individuals, and they too are evidence of divine re-creation. It is a tragedy and a betrayal when such communities are led into conflict with each other through ignorance and the corrupting powers of pride and fear. I believe that all humanity's spiritual traditions recognise a universal kinship between their followers, even if some of them choose to deny it.

Cliff Reed [101]

Since the beginning of Christianity, the unhappy situation in the world has been that the priesthood has been greatly divided and widely separated in their opinion... What can be the reason for so many disagreements? The only reason is that the essential truth is so divided and torn into so many pieces that it is often lost in the strife. One party has truth; another also has some truth, but each thinks it has the whole truth and, therefore, tries to reject that of the other, imagining it is in error.

George de Benneville [102]

We Unitarians should... act as a true friend to Christians, Muslims, and the vast range of other faiths in this country. We share much common ground not just with Muslims and Trinitarian Christians but also with our Jewish and Sikh cousins. This can be seen in a recent statement by Sikhism experts who said that we were their "brother and sisters". We should always look to highlight common ground between us and respect our differences. By nurturing this kind of relationship, we can then come to the table and speak our opposition to actions within a faith if necessary, to engage in honest dialogue and to really start to change the world for the better. This is the true meaning of friendship and one so beautifully shown to us by the Great Exemplar.

Matt Grant [103]

Emerson was one of the first Unitarians to introduce ideas from other religions, principally Hinduism. He tended to use the ideas of the Upanishads and the Bhagavad Gita, rather than to analyse them, undertake authentic exegesis, or expound them systematically. Emerson was one of the first Unitarians to steer the denomination away from an exclusively Christian standpoint and to move towards a position in which all the major world religions are valued, and credited with important insights into religious truth.

George Chryssides [104]

God's care is not limited to those who accept a particular revelation centred on the life and death of Jesus. God's care has resulted in sufficient religious revelation/ guidance [to]... those who have never heard of Jesus... The complexity and depth of Reality have to be seen from various perspectives for a fuller understanding. We, from our limited cultural background, have much to learn by serious encounter with other cultures. I believe that it is NOT true that all religions are saying the same thing, and it is NOT true that all insights are equally valid. But all religions are struggling with the same mysterious, complex reality and have learnt something unique to share with others. This, at least, is part of the perspective of the Universalist.

John Clifford [105]

Study the religions of the world, hearken devoutly to the psalms of the East and to the songs of the West, kneel silently in the temple of the Buddhist, join in the worship of the Jewish synagogue, or listen to the prayers of the Christian Church; in its essence all worship is one, for all religion is one; for all religion leads to God.

Gertrude von Petzold [106]

Part II:
Unitarian Diversity

The religious journeys of different Unitarians will lead to different places. Because of our emphasis on the right of the individual to find her or his own spiritual path, different Unitarians will express their faith differently. Thus there is a great deal of theological and religious diversity in our congregations. Unitarians may express their faith as Christian, post-Christian, theist, humanist, Buddhist, or something else.

Yet in other measures of diversity Unitarians fair less well. In the British Isles Unitarianism remains overwhelmingly a white, middle-class church. This should give us pause for thought. We still have far to go in addressing diversity issues.

Part II surveys Unitarian diversity in terms of theology, sexual orientation, gender identity, race, and ability. It encourages us to think about how diversity both enriches and challenges our faith community.

I am a Christian Unitarian

I am a UU because I believe the freedom to search for truth without the shackles of others' interpretations, opinions and beliefs about God's relationship with man gives me the freedom to love God. I am a Christian because I believe that the ideal for humanity – a world in which we all care for each other and the interdependent web of life – is most possible following Jesus' teachings and ways.

Eileen M. Klees [107]

For me, the supreme affirmation of Christian discipleship is not "I believe" but "I follow."

I cannot wear the "spectacles of faith" and believe in an absolute, unquestioning manner in an exclusive, unique incarnation of the divinity of Jesus.

Jesus to me means following his teaching as an example to live by, something to strive for. Jesus had moments of weakness; he was outraged at social injustice; he showed compassion and understanding to the socially outcast; he could not abide pomposity and worldly show. These attributes reveal his humanity, and so I find myself relating to, and trying to follow his example.

The orthodox presentation of the eternal Christ makes the incarnation a supreme miracle at one point in history. God had revealed himself in man, and that was that; no other human revelation would ever be possible. Whereas I look for, and expect to find, something of the divine within every human being.

Betty Smith [108]

Christianity is not a system of doctrines, but rather a method of attaining oneness with God. It demands, therefore, a good life of piety within, of purity without, and gives the promise that whoso does God's will shall know of God's doctrine.

Theodore Parker [109]

I am a Buddhist Unitarian

[The] blending of Buddhism with Unitarian Universalism began with nineteenth-century Transcendentalists such as Ralph Waldo Emerson and Henry David Thoreau. Unitarian Elizabeth Palmer Peabody translated the first Buddhist text into English. Buddhist reflections about the nature of the world have continued in Unitarian Universalism and have become especially dynamic in recent years.

Western Buddhists of many different schools who are now seeking ways to integrate their experiences of East and West are discovering Unitarian Universalism as a true home...

Many Western Buddhists have been looking for ways to bring our perspectives into the world in a more engaged way... Unitarian Universalism has long been committed to justice and social activism in ways that make sense to many Western Buddhists. Here we found possibilities for enriching our lives and the lives of those we care about.

And, I'm pleased to point out, we Western Buddhists also come bringing gifts. Probably the greatest gift we bring to Unitarian Universalism is meditation. There are a host of practices that might be useful to Unitarian Universalists. Among these are concentration disciplines and the powerful practice of *Metta*, loving kindness. I believe the most important are the practices of pure attention – *Vipassana, Zen,* and *Dzog-chen.* Each is a variation of the original disciplines taught by the Buddha and his immediate followers. Each has to do with simple and plain attention.

Out of this paying attention, bare attention, just noticing, generations of people have found a way through the traps of our dividing consciousness to see that we share a common ground of being. One teacher puts it this way: We are each of us different, stars and people, flies and dirt. But we all belong to the same family. We have a single family name. And that name is the great silence. Sometimes it is called *sunyata*, emptiness.

This is an emptiness that includes all things. We are unique but we are also all of one family. Here we find an ethic that supports Unitarian Universalist longings for moral choice and social justice...

As with all faith traditions encompassed in Unitarian Universalism, it is impossible to describe Unitarian Universalist Buddhism in terms of any one perspective. It is a rich and varied thing we bring into Unitarian Universalism. And the joy for me is that, even as I am transformed by my life as a Unitarian Universalist, I am beginning to see ways in which Unitarian Universalism is transformed by our Buddhist presence.

No one knows where this meeting of East and West in our Unitarian Universalist congregations will lead. Certainly, only time will tell. But the journey is already wonderful and filled with splendid possibilities.

James Ishmael Ford [110]

I am a humanist Unitarian

Through my years of religious education in various Unitarian churches, I felt the affirming love of a religion that had a deep concern for the worth and dignity of all people – including me. I learned to affirm and celebrate life in this world and to work for the betterment of the world and its people. I was nurtured by the feeling that I had the potential and the freedom to experience all kinds of things, to enjoy life and liberty, and to explore many different ideas. I was encouraged to use my mind, to question even the seemingly obvious, and to trust in my own experiences and perceptions.

As I became more involved in the world, I came to value many expressions of the human spirit and the power of human imagination. I appreciate art, music, poetry, drama, and literature. I came to realize that creativity is best nurtured in a climate of freedom where innovation is esteemed. I am glad to have a religion that encourages me to explore and express my aesthetic and sensual side, and to open my heart and mind to the fullness of life in all its aspects.

During the years of my formal education, I particularly valued that Humanism honors reason and encourages integrity. I liked that it invited me to think for myself, to explore, challenge, and doubt; to approach the important questions of life with an openness to new ideas and different perspectives; and then to test these ideas against reality, filter new knowledge through my own active mind, and believe according to the evidence. Humanism provided me with the "tools" I would use to pursue the "free and responsible search for truth and meaning." It invited me to ask about each idea, "Is it reasonable and responsible to believe this? Does it make sense in terms of what is known about the world and the universe?" This is not to suggest that we do not also learn and gain insights from intuition, hunches, flashes of inspiration, even emotion or unexplainable experiences – we do. But when making important decisions that will affect ourselves and others, it behoves us to test our perceptions against reality.

This testing led me to realize that we are all connected to the world, the cosmos, and everything therein. I discovered that Humanism teaches that our well-being and our very existence depend upon the web of life in ways we are only beginning to understand, that our place in nature has to be in harmony with it. Humanism leads me to find a sense of wider relatedness with all the world and its peoples, and it calls me to work for a sound environment and a humane civilization. Because everything is interconnected, I cannot be concerned with my own life and the future of humanity without also being concerned about the future of the planet.

My Humanist religion also prods me to consider the moral principles by which I should live. Humanist ethics, based on love and compassion for humankind and for nature, place the responsibility on humanity for shaping the destiny and future direction of the world. I am called to find my better self and to try to become the best person I can be. Humanism also makes me aware of the existence of moral dilemmas and the need to be very careful and intentional in my moral decision-making, for every decision and action has a consequence now and for the future. I am compelled by my own analysis of the world situation to become involved in service for the greater good of humanity, recognizing that things are changing so quickly that an open-ended approach to solving social problems is needed.

Sarah Oelberg [111]

Many people in atheist and humanist organisations are always talking about people's rights, but never their responsibilities. I cannot accept the existence of a power greater than humans, therefore I am an atheist, but I am not comfortable with the "angry" atheists' self-centred approach. I share the values affirmed by Unitarians, am accepted by them, and am comfortable with their approach to life. I am a Unitarian who is a "religious" atheist.

Anonymous [112]

There is no reason to pitch out humanism now that there is a desire for more spirituality. No parts of our Living Tradition negate or cancel out the others. And I pray (yes, I pray!) that I will not be "drummed out" of humanism because I also call myself a liberal Christian (a follower of the teachings of Jesus), a Zen Buddhist (a believer in the power of presence and paradox) and a pagan (a lover of earthly and natural delights). My style of Unitarian Universalism values theological language, ritual and worship that speaks to the heart and soul as well as to the mind, and ain't I a humanist?

Melanie Morel Sullivan [113]

I am a theist Unitarian

I started attending the Community Church of New York... I learned about the similarities among the great religions of the world, about their common hopes and aspirations for humanity. I heard about the beloved community—the gathered people hungry to do justice and love mercy and walk humbly with God. I heard about people who had risked all they had—even their own lives— in order to speak out loud the longings of their hearts, longings so much like mine.

And I heard about all these things in the context of freedom, the freedom to think for myself about God and about the world, the freedom to decide how I might live so that one day "righteousness and peace would kiss one another," even if I would not live to see that day.

No one required me to make promises I could not keep. There was no list of beliefs that determined whether I was in or out of favor. And most importantly, there were no gatekeepers who decided on my worthiness or unworthiness. Everyone in the sanctuary, including me, was part of a glorious creation. Just by being alive, I was good, I was worthwhile, I was sacred. It was a revelation. For a long time, it was enough—this freedom to think for myself, to embrace the spirit of skepticism and the rejection of doctrine. I reveled in the community of like-minded people, all of us fleeing the excess and rigidity of our childhood beliefs, the blind and unquestioning faith of our fathers and mothers.

But... I kept on living. I kept on living in a world filled with tears and tragic events that had no easy explanations. I kept on facing great joy and deep disappointment. I kept on being confronted by hopeless situations that unexpectedly came to amazing conclusions. And thanks to the freedom I found as a Unitarian Universalist, I continued to ask what it was that I was experiencing.

The answer came slowly. Bit by bit, I learned to acknowledge grace, came to believe the irrational idea that, amid everything, there was a knowing, loving presence that abides in all things, even in me. I knew that I could not explain what was gradually becoming clear to me. I only knew the truth of the mystic Julian of Norwich's proclamation that "all will be well, and all will be well, and all manner of things will be well."

At the same time I was comforted by this notion, I remained suspicious of it. How could all be well when I myself had spent a childhood in which all was definitely not well? How could it all be well as long as people cried out for justice and bread? How could it be well when millions lived out their lives without one moment of ease or pleasure while others knew nothing else? I had no answers to the questions—only the continuing sense that there is so much more to our lives here than the horrors we inflict on one another and the blessings we bestow too rarely.

And then, one day, God spoke. On retreat at a women's conference in Wisconsin, I joined with other participants in a sacred spiral dance led by a noted member of the women's spirituality movement. Asked as part of the dance to speak to the divine and listen for an answer, I joined in, impatient, skeptical, and freezing cold. As I made a perfunctory list of my concerns, I could suddenly feel a Presence in me. It was a Presence that made itself felt in every cell of my body, and it was followed by a Voice, neither male nor female, and utterly unlike anything I had ever felt. The Voice made itself heard in my body, and it told me clearly, lovingly, "Don't worry, my child, don't worry." When I spoke to the Voice about the hopes and dreams of my life, the secret desires I carried with me everywhere, it promised me "all these things and more." And then the Voice and Presence left me, and left me changed forever.

Most of the great Western theologians agree at least on this: God is beyond naming or full understanding, yet we human beings, created in God's image, nonetheless are called to make the attempt. It is the free faith of Unitarian Universalism that makes my attempts worthwhile. Because of this faith, I can be confident that my search for the Divine is structured, not by static institutions or individuals, but by the God who continues to call me and whom I continue to question. Because of this powerful freedom to believe – and to doubt – I live in trust, believing all manner of things will be well.

Rosemary Bray McNatt [114]

Unitarians and sexual and gender diversity

I have been extraordinarily lucky. In living my life as an openly lesbian woman, I have gained far more – infinitely more – than I have lost. One factor tips the balance: I was raised as a Unitarian Universalist. I was raised with Sunday School lessons that taught the beauty of difference, in a faith that nurtures self-respect, dignity, and courage. Most of all, I knew and continue to be affirmed in the truth that no matter what I lost or will lose in coming out, I won't lose my church. I know I am loved not in spite of who or what I am, but because of who and what I am. And that has made all the difference.

Kim K. Crawford Harvie [115]

Each time I tell my story in a Unitarian Universalist congregation, I am met with openness, respect, and caring. Even though many Unitarian Universalists are just learning what it means to be transgender, their response goes well beyond tolerance. Unitarian Universalists consistently yearn to understand, to appreciate, and to welcome my whole story. It is in their company that I have learned that being transgender is a gift.

Sean Dennison [116]

I have been a minister for over twenty years in the same UU congregation, and my church has been very supportive of my partner and myself. They understand that relationships are relationships, gay or straight. What I really like about Unitarian Universalists is that when they find out you're gay, lesbian, or bisexual, they don't react with shock or horror, sympathy or pity, but as if it's the most natural thing in the world, which, of course, it is for us.

Tony Larsen [117]

Three years ago, as a Jew attending a UU Sunday service for the
first time with a friend, I could not have guessed that the following
month I would become a member, six months later I would feel
safe enough to come out as a lesbian, and two years later I would
stand up in a service and announce my upcoming holy union
service! As a Unitarian Universalist I am free to choose my
lifestyle, encouraged to explore my spirituality, and given the
opportunity to learn and grow with people who celebrate diversity.
I feel that I've truly found a home and a family.

Leni Brown [118]

The congregation with which I currently minister is situated in an
urban residential neighbourhood, in the centre of a multi-faith,
multi-cultural, and economically mixed area of the city. Such a
mixture of personal backgrounds puts people into close contact
with individuals who lead lives which are often radically different
from their own.

At its best, my church is a safe haven from prejudice and bigotry,
providing "neutral" territory in which varied community groups
can meet for education, recreation, and worship. I and my partner
of seven years (another man) are welcomed warmly, as a couple,
within the traditional structures of church life. The Unitarian
record of social progress in the area of gay and lesbian tolerance is
well established. It is good to see it in action in my ministry,
wherein I am valued, my relationship is honoured, and no attempt
to deny the reality of gays and lesbians is evident.

Jeffrey Gould [119]

When I first attended this Unitarian church, I found that the
church-sponsored Gay and Lesbian Outreach (GLO) group had
been fostering a climate of queer acceptance for twenty years. I also
found that while the church was strongly welcoming, it wasn't
perfect. As Tom Owen-Towle, one of the parish ministers, once
told me, "We have our warts." I quickly noticed that bisexual

inclusion, or even understanding, was not to be found. It was another opportunity to educate, and my partner and I dreaded the expected long battle to create bi awareness.

We were taken completely by surprise to find people with open minds who would listen, evaluate, and change their minds and hearts. People from both ends of Kinsey's scale [of sexuality] were interested in learning about bisexuality and growing in their understanding and acceptance of all people. I was asked to speak on bisexuality in the church's annual Pride Celebration worship service, and, shortly after, the Gay and Lesbian Outreach committee unanimously agreed to change its name to Rainbow Outreach. After five months, I felt it was time to join the church.

Lynn Dobbs [120]

Unitarians and racial diversity

I attended a social justice workshop where the discussion focused on "What can we do to attract more African Americans to our denomination?" I sensed eyes focusing on me, the only African American present. A woman from Savannah, Georgia, said that her fellowship placed ads in the papers and made attempts to attract African Americans to their group in 1958, but "nobody came." It gave me a sense of joy to tell her that "I came." It took me ten years to join a Unitarian Universalist group in Germany, and now, thirty-three years later, I am a UUA Board member from the district that includes Savannah. I remembered the ads and wondered who were those people called Unitarians and later Unitarian Universalists.

My hope, dream, and wish for us as Unitarian Universalists is that we can embrace pluralism as it is expressed in our Principles and Purposes. I believe that every step or effort toward this goal counts and makes a difference, even if it happens ten or thirty years later. I'm glad I came to Unitarian Universalism and that my friend in Savannah finally learned that her efforts did attract someone.

Leon Spencer [121]

Like so many others, I had been a UU for thirty years without knowing it. We felt immediately at home. I believe there are tens of thousands of Latinos/as who would find religious homes in our churches. I dream not only that our UU churches will learn to reach out and welcome Latinos/as but that some of the strengths of the Hispanic cultures (our love of family, our respect for elders, our sense of community, and our passion for life) will help renew and transform our congregations. Our people need to be welcomed. When they are, they will come bearing gifts.

Peter Morales [122]

Unitarians and ability issues

I speak to you as a woman who is a fully active member of the Unitarian Church... It is only incidentally that I speak to you as a woman who is physically disabled. In other words my argument is going to be that disabled people should be judged primarily by their aptitudes and achievements, just as you would judge an able-bodied person. There should be no place for prejudice...

I have been disabled since birth, but many other people are disabled in later life as a result of accident or illness. Disability is no respecter of persons and can enter the life of any one of us. Therefore, the removal of barriers concerns us all, able-bodied and disabled alike...

In these brief remarks... I do not have time to talk to you about obvious physical barriers, such as flights of stone steps without a hand rail; nor about the personal frustration at having to call for help in everyday situations where the able-bodied among you would find no barrier at all. Rather... I would ask you to reflect that it is in people's minds that we are likely to find the more stubborn barriers, because these barriers often exist as a result of preconceived and deeply rooted ideas or prejudices...

Consider the person and not the disability. Look at the person behind the disability. We disabled people are not simply "wheelchair cases" or "wheelchair bound". We are ordinary people with ordinary needs, although we may use a wheelchair. I would go further. A disabled person is quite likely to have marketable skills in aspects such as independence, organisation, and motivation. These assets come from the need to develop strategies for coping with everyday life...

I put this question to you: are there disabled people within your congregation who seek to be actively involved and yet need encouragement?

My suggestion would be to have one or two individuals in your congregation who might serve as "personal mentors", thereby enabling your disabled members to participate in committee work, for example, or in such everyday duties as taking the collection and making coffee...

I would however go further and argue for the more general recognition that it is up to all of us to... work all the time towards the removal of barriers. Common among these barriers are: unhelpful stereotyping, lack of accessible transport and housing, lack of understanding of our needs and expectations. And over and above these barriers there is one more, and that is prejudice. Such prejudice used to be widespread, and although it has diminished in recent years, there is surely further progress to be made.

Jane Aaronson [123]

Part III:
Unitarian Perspectives

Unitarianism is a creedless faith. However, this does not mean that we have nothing to say about religious, ethical, and political matters. Unitarians continue to struggle with these issues, as individuals and as a community. Unitarians have produced teachings, grounded in our principles, on difficult religious and ethical questions. These teachings continue to guide us in our contemporary reflections and actions, though this does not mean that the issues are closed and not open to further investigation. We are always engaged in spiritual searching and reflection.

Within this spiritual freedom provided by our liberal religious movement Unitarians have, do, and always will come to a number of beliefs, perspectives, opinions, and viewpoints. We should always be involved in conversations about what it means to be human, the best way to live our lives in the world, the nature of the universe, and the heritage bequeathed to us by the world religions.

Part III is an exploration of Unitarian theology and ethics, dealing with human nature, the natural world, God, Jesus, science, and politics. All the voices here deserve our careful consideration as we build our own theology, and work for the Beloved Community.

Human nature and human rights

We may not know what God is, but we can know what it means to be human.

Paul Carnes [124]

The first line of a hymn often sung by Unitarians is "We believe in human kindness". It may seem a trite or sentimental statement with little evidence to back it up, but these few words affirm an essentially religious view of the human condition, without theological presuppositions. For us, humanity's destiny can be a positive one in the next millennium, which need not be determined by the despair and negation which have marked the twentieth century.

Alan Ruston [125]

Unitarianism has held an "enlightened" view of human nature. We have maintained that we can change, are masters of our destinies, and can achieve wholeness. This view I largely endorse – but only if equal weight is given to those aspects of human nature which are deeply embedded in our collective unconscious. We arise from the dynamic interweaving between our needs, urges, and aspirations.

Michaela von Britzke [126]

I can and I must reverence human nature. In its vast potential lie all the attributes of the godlike we may ever know.

William Ellery Channing [127]

We are sinners. About that there is no possible doubt. We have done badly. There is not much doubt about that either. But it is absolutely not true that we are nothing *but* sinners, or that we are drowning in sin and cannot be saved. And it is absolutely not true that we have done nothing but evil and have proved incapable of good. We are good people as well as bad people. And we do good deeds as well as bad deeds. We have done evil things in the world. But we have also done some very good things, even some rather magnificent and generous things. The confession in the Book of Common Prayer that "we have done those things we ought not to have done and left undone those things that we ought to have done" is a large part of the truth. But not all of the truth. And the final clause of that confession, which says that "there is no health in us", is just a mean-spirited lie. There is health in us. And our hope is not in a miracle from the skies, but in the health that is in us! We shall not be defeated by fate; no, if we are defeated, it will only be by letting the health that is in us decay and become a moral sickness.

A. Powell Davies [128]

Man... is not less exclusively a part of nature, than the birds and the plants... He too, like all else, is as the clay to the potter, to be moulded by another; and be the pressure on the inside or on the out, he is shaped and does not shape himself.

James Martineau [129]

Our theological assessment of human nature has been considerably chastened, and we are forced by the facts to live with heightened unease, but as the Reverend Alma Crawford reminds us: "Discomfort, like prayer, fasting, and yoga, can become a spiritual discipline." Our cheerful band of religious liberals must now practice our faith in light of human behavior that is incurably ambiguous, complex and varied. Everyone, including ourselves, is capable of both deep caring and destructive aggression, moments of the sublime and the bestial. All our solid thinking, mystical consciousness, and benevolent hands can diminish but never fully dislodge evil.

Tom Owen-Towle [130]

The belief that there are natural rights that all people may justly claim relied, in the end, upon religion. This is not to say that they rely upon some particular creed or that their basis is dogmatic, but only that they cannot be credibly asserted except upon the assertion that human nature is moral and spiritual, and that we so accept it. Wherever this assumption is rejected, it quickly becomes evident that there is no right but might: whatever prevails does so because there are those who have the power to enforce it...

[When] we are in peril, some of these rights – so we are told – must be curtailed. Very well. It may be so. But at least, let us see that their curtailment is not just a matter of procedure, an external device to protect our security: it is a deep injury to human nature itself and lowers the level of the one society we are trying to make secure... From the standpoint of religion, it profanes the sacred; it sins against the human soul, the breath of the spirit of God.

A. Powell Davies [131]

Feminism and Unitarianism

There is no work in the world, except perhaps the slaughtering of
other people, that a woman cannot do as efficiently as a man if she
is given the same training and opportunity.

Gertrude von Petzold [132]

We take a pride in claiming that ours was the first denomination to
accept women into its ministry. England's first woman minister,
the Rev Gertrude von Petzold, was inducted into the ministry of
Narborough Road Free Christian Church, Leicester, in 1904, but
the Unitarian Church in Glasgow does have a prior claim. In its
earlier days as a Universalist Church, the Rev Caroline Soule was
there ordained in 1880. Close links with Unitarians enabled her to
preach in and later have temporary pastoral oversight of the
Dundee Unitarian Church.

Celia Kerr [133]

Looking back over 40 years, I now realise that my own awareness
of my worth and spirituality as a woman was stimulated through
the words, influence and personal example of a woman, a
Unitarian minister. Over the years other Unitarians have
continued to feed my spiritual needs, but this woman shines out.

In 1953 I first attended a service in a Unitarian church. I had tested
several denominations, but none seemed to satisfy whatever it was
that I needed. I did not know what I was seeking. I was 21 years old
and lacking in self-confidence, and here I was in a church which
emphasised the worth in all and no guilt feelings about sin and
salvation. I was hearing about the humanity of Jesus of Nazareth
and the divinity in all humankind. So God was not watching and
judging me. What blessed relief. And a woman in the pulpit, this
was something really new. I had discovered a church which offered
a reasonable, sensitive, relevant and encouraging approach to
religion. I responded to all this.

Vina Curren [134]

Through Unitarianism I have developed my kind of feminism, that men and women are essentially different, but complementary, that both sexes should value these differences, and at the same time realise that we all have within us both masculine and feminine qualities that need expression. Most fundamentally, that God is neither male nor female, neither god nor goddess.

Irene Hornby [135]

Having reached the position of General Assembly President, a post held by ten other women since 1928, I am very much aware that I have achieved more than I could in most religious denominations. When friends outside the movement learn the reason for my increased activity this year, they are invariably surprised that I, a laywoman, should fill such a role...

One of the things I have always valued in my experience of the Unitarian movement is the sense of being treated as a person in my own right – not just as someone's wife, mother, or daughter. During the last fifteen years I have worked at home, caring for my husband and step-family of five children and have at times felt that in catering for their genuinely substantial needs I was completely losing track of my own personality. For me, sharing in worship with Edinburgh Unitarians is a revitalising experience in which my own sense of identity is restored.

Focusing attention upon the needs of my inner self gives me a perspective on daily living which recognises the importance of my own feelings and opinions in relation to those of other people, against the backdrop of eternity.

I find the general sensitivity in our churches to the use of gender-exclusive language very helpful, because I believe God to be neither male nor female; surely the Power of Goodness, Beauty, Truth, and Love has the attributes of both sexes? As one who feels excluded by language which seems to imply that God speaks only to "the sons of men", I really do appreciate those who avoid its usage. This shared outlook enables me to affirm the value of women and women's experience in society.

Celia Kerr [136]

Tonight I repent of my smugness. Tonight I acknowledge that I speak to you as a recovering sexist among recovering sexists who share membership in a religious institution which still has far to go before resting on any laurels. I speak in the spirit of the Polish Unitarians of the mid-seventeenth century who wrote in a new preface to their catechism: "We do not think that we ought to be ashamed if in some respect our church improves."

Katharine Winthrop [137]

Nature and ecology

Freedom, reason, tolerance, and pluralism are not, of course, adequate components of a religious faith in and of themselves – they can only provide the context in which faith can emerge, evolve, and live. Within its pluralism, Unitarianism will doubtless continue to take many theological and philosophical forms during the next century. However, a broad consensus may well be evolving around a principle expressed in the UUA covenant as "respect for the interdependent web of all existence of which we are a part". Significantly, at least one Transylvanian minister has asserted that this principle well embodies his own theology. Perhaps the traditional affirmation of *Egy az Isten* – God is One! – will point beyond itself and, while the nature of the Creator may remain a mystery, the Oneness of the Creation may become increasingly manifest.

Charles A. Howe [138]

I do not think I understand the meaning of the word *spiritual*, but my new and first ever prescription sunglasses may have given me some insight. The old railway, now cycle path that I bounce along to my work, glows with the vigour of urgent unruly plant life in colours subtly new and unexpected. Mysterious greens, yellows vividly old gold, pinks faded and matured make work seem less important, so I stop to ponder my response. Why does this loveliness tug at me so? I understand, since life's key is protein, that my proteins are responding to the effects of those around me. And proteins have their own beauty, not merely that of their occasional weird symmetries, but a supreme intellectual beauty. Each atom of the thousands in one molecule is precisely placed by a turmoil of balanced weak forces so that the molecule may do its job: an apparent triumph of design. And did this arise blindly, through occasional tiny errors frozen by selection, the huge majority discarded? And how did it begin? And why do I respond to Nature with this strange yearning, this "calm so deep"? But it's not at all calm, more like a huge excitement bubbling in my depths too far down to analyse. Is it MY proteins creating God in me? Why? I start euphorically greeting bewildered strangers. Does this response enhance the survival of my genes? I don't see how! I don't see why!

Simon Hardy [139]

It is a religious requirement to try to live in such a way as not to cause unnecessary damage to this world, nor to prevent other people from enjoying their fair share of the earth's resources. I try not to waste these resources and avoid unnecessary consumption, though my Western lifestyle makes this difficult. This means using my car as little as possible (I have not yet managed to change my life enough to do without it), thinking twice about what I buy, re-using envelopes and plastic bags, recycling what waste I can.

Where possible I buy goods which have been produced in a way that is sensitive to the environment and fair to the producers. I use Traidcraft or Oxfam tea, coffee, muesli, etc., and recycled toilet rolls and paper. For years I avoided South African fruit, and now I try to take the advice given in *The Ethical Consumer* about which brands to use or avoid. I am a vegetarian. Shopping and eating are both expressions of my religious concern.

Gardening helps to make part of the environment beautiful and is also a source of spiritual renewal. If I feel distressed, depressed, or overburdened, a couple of hours' work in the garden usually brings a sense of consolation, and grounds my spirit in the underlying creativity and rhythm of existence.

People, like plants, come in various forms; we all have much in common, but we also have our individual needs and gifts. Some plants spread vigorously and have to be cut back in order to give others room to grow. This is a salutary parable for privileged Westerners.

Ann Peart [140]

The facts about the plight of the earth are well documented, but our political and economic structures have yet to learn the error of their unsustainable ways. Behind these structures are ordinary people – like you and me – who benefit from the system and complain if we are asked to make sacrifices.

Our civilisation now has a profoundly flawed relationship with the planet. This has grave implications for the future and a severe impact in the present, with the world's poor paying the price for our wasteful and destructive ways. We need to focus on those spiritual resources which could yet restore humanity's vision and the earth's fortunes. Most cultures see in the universe the work of an ultimate or divine reality, and teach that our well-being depends on maintaining a right relationship with the creation and the divine power that called it into being.

In the Judaeo-Christian tradition the true relationship of humanity with the earth is best stated in the Genesis creation myth, where Adam – created out of the same "dust of the ground" as all the plants and animals – is given a specific task: "The Lord God took the man and put him in the garden of Eden to till it and to care for it." Thus humanity's role is to be earth's gardener and curator, with the responsibility for looking after those who share this garden-planet with us.

The theme of our intimate relationship with a sacred creation recurs throughout the Bible: from God's covenant with Noah "and with all living creatures" (Gen. 9: 12–17), through Psalm 104's hymn of praise for God's handiwork, and the prophet's vision of cosmic harmony in the Messianic age (Is. 11: 6–9); to Jesus' lyrical invocation of "the birds of the air.... the lilies of the field" (Matt. 6: 26–30), and Paul's perception that nature is transparent with the divine "to the eye of reason" (Rom. 1: 19–20).

The message that creation is sacred and that we must be its good stewards should be incorporated into our worship, our politics, our economics and our individual lifestyles.

Cliff Reed [141]

I do not see human beings as the ultimate crown of creation. Life forms do not constitute a pyramid with humans at the apex, but rather a circle where everything is connected and interdependent. We could not live without the rest of nature, but nature can carry on without us!

Anne Cameron writes, "We all have a right to live on this Earth. We have the right to be free and to live in balance with nature, a part of nature, not apart from nature. We have the right not to be separated from our Mother, and we have the duty and obligation not to have our Mother destroyed..." We need a holistic approach, with the goal of establishing a balance among all the different communities that comprise the living body of our Mother earth.

I do not subscribe to the dualist presupposition which makes a division between spirit and matter, mind and body, culture and nature. I believe earth-based spirituality can help to heal this perceived split by celebrating the cycle of life – birth, growth, maturity, decay, death, and re-birth – as it manifests in the seasonal round of the year, in the phases of the moon and in human, plant, and animal life. Celebrating the cycles of nature is very important to me. Together with others, I have reclaimed ancient rituals at the solstices and equinoxes, affirming my connectedness to the changing cycles of the seasons. By attuning to the passing seasons my life takes on a new vitality.

Ingrid Tavkar [142]

Although his roots were in Unitarian Christianity, Ralph Waldo Emerson's own theology was pantheistic, having been greatly influenced by Plato and the Hindu scriptures. Consequently he saw the world both as an emanation from God, within whom "every man's particular being is contained and made one with all other...and to which every part and particle is equally related" and also as "one vast picture which God paints on eternity". All created things therefore have an equally important role.

Even though we may be unconscious of it, the doctrine of creation which belongs to our inherited or adopted faith makes a great difference to how we value and relate to the world around us. A God who creates the world out of nothing is essentially apart from that world. A God whose very substance forms the universe is totally involved in that universe. He cannot punish or destroy any part of it without doing violence to himself. Neither can we. It seems to me that only this second option, pantheism, can lead to a true concern for the natural world. Once we realise that all matter is divine, that all living things are divine, then (and only then) will we respect them.

Rosemary Griffith [143]

A man is really ethical only when he obeys the constraint laid on him to help all life which he is able to succour, and when he goes out of his way to avoid injuring anything living. He does not ask how far this or that life deserves sympathy as valuable in itself, nor how far it is capable of feeling. To him life as such is sacred. He shatters no ice crystal that sparkles in the sun, tears no leaf from its tree, breaks off no flower, and is careful not to crush any insect as he walks...

He is not afraid of being laughed at as sentimental. It is indeed the fate of every truth to be an object of ridicule when it is first acclaimed. It was once considered foolish to suppose that coloured men were really human beings and ought to be treated as such. What was once foolishness has now become a recognized truth. Today it is considered as exaggeration to proclaim constant respect for every form of life as being the serious demand of a rational ethic. But the time is coming when people will be amazed that the human race was so long before it recognized thoughtless injury to life as incompatible with real ethics. Ethics is in its unqualified form extended responsibility with regard to everything that has life...

Thought becomes religious when it thinks itself out to the end. The ethic of reverence for life is the ethic of Jesus brought to philosophical expression, extended into cosmic form, and conceived as intellectually necessary.

Albert Schweitzer [144]

What is sacred?

Whatever I can appreciate of God (however I understand this), or of value and concern, is to be sought in this world. I find it through what I can experience by my senses – what I can see, hear, touch, smell and taste. So the sacred is available in the details of everyday life. Some people talk of the world as "God's body", and I respond to this.

Ann Peart [145]

Religion consists of those actions, purposes, and experiences which are humanly significant. Nothing human is alien to the religious. It includes labor, art, science, philosophy, love, friendship, recreation – all that is in its degree expressive of intelligently satisfying human living. The distinction between the sacred and the secular can no longer be maintained.

"A Humanist Manifesto" 1933 [146]

No greater discovery is given to our kind
than to realise our divinity.
That ordinary morning walk through the park
where in an extraordinary moment of wondrous light
the truth may dawn
that-I-and-thee-and-we-and-tree are One.
And if this weren't enough, even more
this Oneness is immensely Powerful,
an empowering and transforming Love.
For all the good we may choose to achieve from this knowing
    Oneness,
Sky Father, Earth Mother, we are thankful.

Alistair Bate [147]

God

Question with boldness even the existence of a God; because, if there be one, he must more approve of the homage of reason, than that of blindfolded fear... Do not be frightened from this inquiry by any fear of its consequences. If it ends in a belief that there is no God, you will find incitements to virtue in the comfort and pleasantness you feel in its exercise, and the love of others which it will procure you. If you find reason to believe there is a God, a consciousness that you are acting under his eye, and that he approves you, will be a vast additional incitement.

Thomas Jefferson [148]

We believe in the doctrine of God's unity, or that there is one God, and one only... We believe in the moral perfection of God... We cannot bow before a being, however great and powerful, who rules tyrannically... We believe God is infinitely good... not to a few, but to all; good to every individual.

William Ellery Channing [149]

The universe, and humanity within it, constitutes an indivisible, universal, and organic whole. Having basically the same elements and structures everywhere, the universe is homogeneous, with the same substance and laws found throughout...

Why is the universe unified and indivisible? That question may be answered in theological language. Because its creator and preserver, God, is also one and indivisible, in essence and function. God is a unity because only the world itself is unity. If God's being was even minimally divided, nature would also immediately divide, losing its characteristic unity and relative identity. However, from both logical and experiential viewpoints, this is a transparent absurdity. God is one because the world is one, and vice versa. God is indivisible because the world is also indivisible, and vice versa. This is not merely an analogy but a result of logical and empirical experience.

Imre Gellérd [150]

Associating myself with the spiritual force in the universe adds to my own power to make a contribution to it. I prefer not to say "God" because there are so many varying definitions which could make for disagreement. Theists like myself can supply it in their minds.

Raymond B. Johnson [151]

Unitarian Universalists tend to be, whether they like the word or not, agnostics. We simply do not know for a certainty. We are not anti-God, and few of us would call ourselves atheists, although since we are a non-creedal church there is nothing to rule out an atheist being a Unitarian Universalist.

George N. Marshall [152]

When I am asked if I believe in God, I am either impatient or amused and frequently decline to reply. All I know, all I want to know is that I have found in my relationships with my fellow men and in my glad beholding of the universe a reality of truth, goodness, and beauty, and that I am trying to make my life as best as I can a dedication to this reality. When I am in a thinking mood, I try to be rigorously rational and, thus, not to go one step further in my thoughts and language than my reason can take me. I then become uncertain as to whether I or any one can assert much about God and fall back content into the mood of Job. When, however, in preaching or in prayer, in some high moment of inner communion or a profound experience with life among my fellows, I feel the pulse of emotion suddenly beating in my heart and I am lifted up as though upon some sweeping tide that is more than the sluggish current of my days, I find it easier to speak as the poets speak and cry, as so many of them cry, to God.

But when I say "God," it is poetry and not theology. Nothing that any theologian ever wrote about God has helped me much, but everything that poets have written about flowers and birds and skies and seas and the saviors of the race and God – whosoever he may be – has at one time or another reached my soul! More and more, as I grew older, I live in the lovely thought of these seers and prophets. The theologians gather dust upon the shelves of my library, but the poets are stained with my fingers and blotted with my tears. I never seem so near truth as when I care not what I think or believe, but only with these masters of inner vision would live forever.

John Haynes Holmes [153]

I believe that there is one most High God, Creator of Heaven and Earth, and first Cause of all things pertaining to our Salvation, and consequently the ultimate Object of our Faith and Worship; and that this God is none but the Father of our Lord Jesus Christ.

John Biddle [154]

I grow in God. I am only a form of him. He is the soul of me. I can even with mountainous aspiring say, I am God.

Ralph Waldo Emerson [155]

God (or that in which we may have faith) is the inescapable, commanding reality that sustains and transforms all meaningful existence... God is that reality which works upon us and through us and in accord with which we can achieve truth, beauty, or goodness. It is that creativity which works in nature and history, under certain conditions creating human good in human community.

James Luther Adams [156]

God is as close to us as we are to ourselves.

Marjorie Newlin Leaming [157]

Every picture of God is a self-portrait.

J. Frank Schulman [158]

Goodbye, dear Lord and Father.
I have loved you, but cannot hold you any longer;
You are departing from me, your image is fading away.
How can I call you Father when I am told that
I am created in your image?
Your power has kept me all these years, but now I have grown up
  and I must leave you.

I must redeem my connection to all of creation and affirm the lost
  wholeness.
I too have been called to be responsible for the world, the earth, the
  cosmos and myself.
I too am related to the "big" words: calling, suffering, creation, and
  knowledge.
I am part of the "Dance of being," in me lives the spirit of passion
  and compassion!

Oh, I still love you, but it's not the same.
You must leave me now, so that you can come back to me as a new
  being.
So please, Lord Father .... vanish!

Come God, mysterious presence, dynamic and driving power in
  the cosmos, tempting and inviting voice of love and justice ....

Welcome!

Johanna Boeke [159]

I, a preacher, who talks of him with varying vigour each Sunday morning, who prays to him in a kind of hopeless hoping for cancer-afflicted friends, I hear the consuming confident cry of the convert "I have found God."

I hear also the quieter reflection based on sadder musings: "Sometimes he hides himself most wondrously as though there were no God."

Have I discovered him – have I looked hard enough or merely a casual glance at the table and an anguished howl, "Where have you put the keys!" Where did I leave God the last time I stopped using him. Where did someone else take him when they needed him.

Glimpses come and go – a 1,000 year old church ringing to David Bowie for the life of an 18 year old, life ended at 18 which should have gone on forever.

And perhaps it does – with God discovering while I am still searching, with an off-hand casualness until the next grief of pain.

Has God discovered me yet? I am not one of those whose circle in the pavement of Philippi indicates that I died for him. The anguish, the loss, the pain of Belsen were not mine.

I too have hidden myself most wondrously as though there were no me.

Has God discovered me? Or am I a formless speck among millions? Has he who sees the sparrow fall marked on some chart with dots of red or green or blue depicting the distribution of sparrows discovered me?

Lena Cockroft [160]

There is no God in the sky: God is in the heart that loves the sky's blueness.

A. Powell Davies [161]

What is our concept of the divine, or that which is of ultimate concern? In most congregations God is still referred to more often as male than female, for example when the Lord's Prayer is said or sung, beginning with the invocation to "Our Father". Rarely is this counterbalanced with equal references to the divine as female, though gender-neutral terms are often used. While the divine is thought of as more male than female, women will have a lower status than men, and we will have more difficulty valuing ourselves as subjects (rather than objects).

Ann Peart [162]

He [Theodore Parker] prayed to the Creator, the infinite Mother of us all (always using Mother instead of Father in this prayer). It was the prayer of all I ever heard in my life which was the truest to my individual soul.

Barbara Leigh Smith Bodichon [163]

Jesus

Jesus Christ... is a true man by nature, as the holy Scriptures frequently testify concerning that matter... whatsoever divine excellency Christ hath, the Scripture testifieth that he hath it by gift of the Father... the Scripture doth most evidently shew, that Jesus Christ doth perpetually ascribe all his Divine acts not to himself, or any Divine of his own, but to the Father.

Racovian Catechism (Faustus Socinus) [164]

Jesus is a multidimensional figure. He stands in the prophetic line of Judaism, and for those who would be his followers he opens up the rich tradition of the Hebrew Scriptures... The words and deeds of Jesus recorded in the New Testament provide the blueprint for human fulfillment. Jesus calls us to comfort and sustain one another, to lift the burden of the oppressed, and to serve God with joy.

Judith L. Hoehler [165]

While Jesus was, like all people, a unique individual, he was not other than human. He was our brother in every sense, sharing the same human lineage as us. And thus when we speak of him as child of God, as incarnate divinity, as vessel of God's promise to humankind, we speak of him as embodiment, as symbol of what is true of every human baby.

The ministry of Jesus, and of those who have walked the same path, was indeed an enfleshment of creative power, supremely that of love, which can re-make human beings by revealing to them their roots in a divine creation, their reclaimable goodness and wholeness, their oneness with this glorious universe.

Cliff Reed [166]

Jesus' life was not bounded by the time, the county or the community in which it was lived, for he knew and lived by the truths that are valid always and everywhere. Although many have thought to excuse their own dismal failures by calling him visionary and impractical, they have known in their hearts that it was they who were impractical, for everything that they have touched has turned to ashes.

It is true that Jesus knew nothing of the modern conditions of life. He never saw a factory or heard its clatter. He never listened to a radio or watched television or rode in an automobile. He never visited a hospital or worked in a scientific laboratory. But these are only the gadgets of life! Life itself Jesus knew. Birth and death, work and wages, sickness and despair, poverty and blessings and hardships that make up life are not new to us. They were not new in his day. They have been present in every age. Every human goodness and evil, dream and failure which we know he also knew. He spoke to a world like ours. Despite our unwillingness to pay the price of discipleship, we believe in him, not because he was God, but because he was man, at man's best.

Robert Killam [167]

I believe that Jesus Christ, to the intent that he might be our Brother, and have a Fellow-feeling of our Infirmities, and so become more ready to help us, (the consideration whereof, is the greatest Encouragement to Piety that might be imagined) hath no other than a Human Nature.

John Biddle [168]

Jesus Christ belonged to the true race of prophets. He saw with open eye the mystery of the soul. Drawn by its severe harmony, ravished with its beauty, he lived in it, and had his being there. Alone in all history he estimated the greatness of man. One man was true to what is in you and me. He saw that God incarnates himself in man, and evermore goes forth anew to take possession of his World. He said in this jubilee of sublime emotion, "I am divine. Through me, God acts; through me, speaks. Would you see God, see me; or see thee, when thou also thinkest as I now think."

Ralph Waldo Emerson [169]

[Jesus'] authentic words and deeds were designed to enable people, in a radically open-ended fashion, to come to life *as they were* and not to impose on them a single, fixed response to the world. Jesus did not teach a complete theology or philosophy; by offering what one might call *a practical doctrine of life*, he suggested how we might achieve genuine mindfulness...

The teachings of Jesus inspire us to ask the right questions. He does not achieve this by delineating precisely what he has seen, but instead suggests to us that our relationship with the ground of being is filial in nature (our *Father*), and that we experience this relationship most fully in the context of a "place" called the Kingdom of God. Jesus seems to suggest thereby that "God" (the *one*) and the "Kingdom of God" (the *many*) are intimately and necessarily connected. This person/place, he tells us, is *like a man who sowed a seed on the earth... like a mustard seed... like yeast... like an empty jar... like a treasure buried in a field... like a merchant looking for fine pearls*, and (perhaps most tellingly) that *it is within* (or *in your presence*)...

The teachings of Jesus allow us to recognise and explain in clear and beautiful ways that in our own diverse and inclusive communities all individuals, when they *come as they are*, can be parables of the Kingdom of Heaven; although as apparently different from each other as mustard seeds are from pearls, we affirm that we are somehow the same. The practical vision of diversity and unity, of the many acting as one, is precisely what the contemporary Unitarian community aims to realise.

Andrew Brown [170]

Jesus stood both in the prophetic tradition of such figures as Isaiah and Hosea, and in the kingly line of David. His ministry took place in a primarily Jewish context. His challenge to a corrupt priesthood in the Jerusalem Temple made him powerful enemies. These found common cause with the ruthless Roman authorities. The result was his crucifixion, a supreme example of human integrity and faithfulness in the face of human evil. Unitarians do not see the crucifixion as a blood sacrifice for sin.

Whatever Jesus' own perception, his followers – like him, all faithful Jews – believed him to be the Messiah, "the anointed one"; in Greek, "the Christ".

Today's Unitarians are not first-century Jews. We cannot share their perspective. However, Jesus' teachings and what we know of his life lead Unitarians to regard him as a major (some would say the major) figure in humanity's spiritual journey. While honouring him, we do not worship him, something we believe he would not have wanted.

Cliff Reed [171]

The Bible

Unitarians see the Bible as the record of a people's long struggle to understand themselves, their world and their God. In it the writers describe and interpret the spiritual dimension of their existence and their history. In the insights, stories, and experiences that the Bible's human authors record, we can learn much in our own quest for faith and meaning.

Where we find in scripture a source of sustaining and abiding truth, it can be said to be a source of divine wisdom. But Unitarians do not approach the Bible uncritically or without discrimination. Nor do we regard it as an inerrant and unquestionable authority. What it says must be viewed in the light of reason and conscience. Due regard must be given to the continuing discoveries of biblical criticism, serious scholarship, and archaeology.

Anything in the Bible that Unitarians accept as true is accepted because it rings true in our own humble reflection upon it. We do not accept it just because it is in the Bible. Much that is there is clearly addressed to particular cultural and historical situations. Much belongs to a remote stage of religious development to which we cannot relate.

Taking the advice of Paul the Apostle, Unitarians prefer to abide by the spirit of the Bible's sacred treasures than by a narrow adherence to the letter.

Cliff Reed [172]

Oppressive interpretations of the Bible do kill, literally.... Massive injustice has been and continues to be done in the name of the Bible. But the problem is not simply with or within religion. The problem is that all of us allow powers and principalities of both secular and spiritual oppression to usurp the spirit of the Bible and use it to legitimize such clear sins as economic and environmental exploitation, racism, sexism, homophobia, and more...

Those who reject or neglect the Bible fail to recognize that to "throw the Bible out" because others have turned it into an idol, or because you don't accept what you take to be the conventional understanding of its teachings, doesn't mean that it ever goes away. Rather it simply means that it ends up only in the hands and on the lips of others – often reactionary others – where it can and will be used against you.

John Buehrens [173]

Science and technology

Man loves to wonder, and that wonder is the seed of his science.

Ralph Waldo Emerson [174]

Of all the paths derived from Christianity, Unitarianism has an approach to investigating spiritual truths that is closest to the scientific method for discovering and elucidating material truths. Furthermore, most Unitarians are curious about spiritual matters and excited by the idea that there is more to be discovered, just as scientists are curious about nature.

Simon Hardy [175]

[Joseph] Priestley was motivated to study science as an exploration of the Creation. Our modern motivation may be expressed in different words, but amounts to much the same thing: the curiosity we feel about the Universe in which we live is quite compelling. The quest of exploration of the Universe and the matter of which it is composed is essentially a religious endeavour, requiring energy, commitment, and – most of all – imagination.

David Williams [176]

If work on the Human Genome Project goes according to plan, within a couple of decades we shall have identified all the major genes from the 100,000 or so on each of the 23 pairs of human chromosomes. This raises the issue of how far our behaviour is predetermined; not a new question, of course, but one given more meaning as we come to understand the scope and fine details of our genetic instructions. Certainly we are not pre-programmed robots: many of the genetic instructions result in a tendency for certain things to happen given specific environmental factors (some of which are under our control). Furthermore, most known instructions concern physiological processes; the way we actually behave is more complicated and results from a much larger number of genes and a side range of environmental influences. In other words, we usually do have a choice.

Genetic engineering opens up exciting possibilities: for example, we now know a great deal about how genes control the antibodies which form our immune system, and it might soon be a routine matter to repair accidental deficiencies. The most sensitive issue of all is cloning, but human cloning of the sort that produced Dolly the sheep is not legally sanctioned and this is unlikely to change. However, the cloning of human tissues for use in transplant surgery (for example, skin which could be produced to be more compatible with burn victims) is a realistic possibility.

These and similar ethical issues must surely concern all Unitarians, who have a long tradition of trying to make up their own minds to arrive at rational decisions. The most important challenge to any religious preconceptions comes not from the facts of genetic advances but from the associated ideas that have been generated. Richard Dawkins' contention that human beings are not simply organisms that happen to have genes, but rather that our bodies are just convenient homes in which our genes pursue their own evolutionary destiny, is a fascinating challenge to all religions and needs to be seriously addressed.

Derrick Pritchatt [177]

What... should a Unitarian perspective on genetic modification [GM] be?

First, not to be dogmatic and not to adopt a simple sweeping solution to a complex problem. A total ban on genetic modification, because it is God's work and not ours, would be one such solution. But why is it God's work, and who decides that it is? A similar argument has been used against innumerable innovations that are now commonplace, for example against the alleviation of the pain of childbirth with anaesthetics, and against travelling faster than a horse can run!

Second, not to accept criticisms of capitalism and its methods as criticisms of genetic modification. Much of the anti-GM argument has been criticism of false advertising, aggressive marketing, economic bullying, and the like. Such criticism of genetic modification is like arguing that because drug addicts use injection, all injections should be prohibited.

Third, to be thoughtful: to consider each GM organism separately, and consider critically whether it will bring benefits, whether it is dangerous, and whether the predicted benefits are likely to outweigh the foreseen dangers. We can test for the benefits and dangers, provided eco-terrorists permit it. Unforeseen dangers we cannot allow for, except by banning the development and use of any GM organism.

Should we decide that this last is our best policy and we enforce it in the developing world by economic or other means, then we must accept that from our comfortable and luxurious lives we are depriving others of predictable benefits, sometimes of life itself, because of a primitive fear of the unknown. This seems to me to be both immoral and the very antithesis of the Unitarian approach summarised in that first verse of the hymn "Joy of Living": "*Of searching, doubting, testing, Of deeper insights gained.*"

Simon Hardy [178]

The name of Tim Berners-Lee, who devised the World Wide Web, is little known to the public. Interestingly, Berners-Lee is a Unitarian... [He] sees parallels between Unitarianism and the way the World Wide Web operates: both are networks which allow freedom to explore ideas, and toleration of conflicting opinions...

In the main, the vast majority of Unitarians have maintained the spirit of welcoming intellectual inquiry and technological innovation, and they perceive the Web as an important tool for disseminating liberal religion, for developing the movement's ideas, and for obtaining a platform from which potentially to communicate with the rest of the world.

Tony Cann and George Chryssides [179]

It is the scientists who originate and develop knowledge of the physical world, enabling people to improve their lives through advancing technologies. However, material transformations initiated by some new concept or discovery may not necessarily benefit humans or the world around them; sometimes they end up harming them. Nor do we always use information that scientists have gathered through the centuries to improve our health or the way we live together. More than ever before, scientists should propose ideas for achieving the optimum health of that prime human invention – the social organism called society.

Linus Pauling [180]

Politics and democracy

Pray with your ballots!

Susan B. Anthony [181]

Inasmuch as these matters [social, economic, and environmental justice] are political in the broadest sense, then Unitarians do mix religion with politics. This means, for some, active involvement in campaigns, marches and demonstrations. It may mean lobbying politicians and making legislators aware of Unitarian concerns in particular areas of policy. It means using one's democratic rights responsibly and purposefully for the common good. It means focusing on political and social issues in worship in order to explore their spiritual implications.

Cliff Reed [182]

Liberals think of Democracy not only as freedom and equality of opportunity, but also as mutual assistance in the use of freedom and opportunity. To take one class off the shoulder of another class is not enough. All people must work shoulder to shoulder.

Curtis W. Reese [183]

In almost every case, it is only by legislation (as you all know) that the *roots* of great evils can be touched at all and that the social diseases of pauperism and vice and crime can be brought within hope of cure. Women, with the tenderest hearts and best intentions, go on labouring all their lifetimes often in merely pruning the offshoots of these evil roots, in striving to allay and abate the symptoms of the disease. But the nobler and much more truly philanthropic work of plucking up the roots, or curing the disease, they have been forced to leave to men.

Frances Power Cobbe [184]

I have grave reservations about liberal democracy as it is known and practiced in contemporary life, especially the life of our modern industrial and consumer way of life, masquerading as liberal democracy. The fate of the earth hinges upon our heeding voices such as those of Thoreau... and awakening to the meaning of liberal democracy as a comprehensive personal, social, and religious faith...

In recent years there has also appeared a major post-Marxist critique of liberal democracy that holds it responsible not for the world's progress, but for most of its problems – including its environmental problems...

What these critiques add up to is an indictment of liberal democracy as a philosophy of citizenship adequate to the ecological age. Liberal democracy does not promote equal, free, and mutual participation of all persons in politics, business, and culture, but instead limits the role of citizenship to choosing which elite will govern them. Everything else is left to what is called 'society': that freewheeling, amorphous region of mass public opinion, voluntary association, and individual pursuit of economic gain... Liberal democracy is not, in other words, democratic, in the essential and enduring sense of democracy as "the power of the people to govern themselves"....

If we accept the burden of this critique, as I do, we are left with a dilemma. To continue to support liberal democratic values and institutions is to undercut the positive understanding of citizenship necessary to address the global ecological crisis. But to reject liberal democracy is to cut ourselves off from the most successful democratic tradition in the world today, and its precious inheritance of human rights, reason, and government under law – an inheritance more precious, we must add, with every passing day...

There is, however, another view of liberal democracy, and another experience of it – one based on a strong, communal understanding of citizenship and our interdependence with the rest of life, which at the same time affirms the essential liberal principles of individual freedom and reason. We may call this radical, revolutionary, or prophetic liberal democracy.

J. Ronald Engel [185]

The democratic process is an act of faith: not faith that any one point of view will prevail, but faith that the will of the people will point us toward the Beloved Community.

William G. Sinkford [186]

War and peace

On pacifism, as on all issues of personal conscience, each Unitarian is free to come to his or her own conclusions without fear of judgment or censure. So although there are many Unitarian pacifists, there is no explicit requirement or implicit expectation on the matter. Unitarians live with diversity and its potential tensions – on this subject as on many others. A Unitarian congregation may include both pacifists and members of the armed forces.

But whether pacifist or not, Unitarians affirm the values of peace, justice, forgiveness, and reconciliation. Some call these divine values. They are held to be necessary for the wholeness and happiness of any human community, from the family to the nation and the world.

On the subject of war, Unitarians agree that it is wrong. Some say that this rules out the use of force entirely, that it can never be justified in any situation. For others, though, there are – sadly, tragically – situations in which the use of proportionate force is necessary in order to prevent or defeat a greater evil, particularly to defend the innocent and the weak in immediate peril.

Cliff Reed [187]

Throughout their history, Unitarians have been notable for advocating the extension of the franchise to all men and to women, and for the extension of education similarly; they have campaigned against slavery and racism; they have pioneered public health reforms; and in modern times they have advocated equality for those whose sexual orientation differed from the statistical norm. Their traditional strong emphasis on human rights, however, has not led to a general rejection of war. Yet war is surely the greatest violation of human rights imaginable.

George Paxton [188]

Arise then, women of this day!

Arise all women who have hearts, whether your baptism be that of water or of fears!

Say firmly: "We will not have great questions decided by irrelevant agencies, our husbands shall not come to us, reeking with carnage, for caresses and applause. Our sons shall not be taken from us to unlearn all that we have been able to teach them of charity, mercy and patience. We women of one country will be too tender of those of another country to allow our sons to be trained to injure theirs."

From the bosom of the devastated earth a voice goes up with our own. It says, "Disarm, Disarm!" The sword of murder is not the balance of justice! Blood does not wipe out dishonour, nor violence indicate possession.

As men have often forsaken the plow and the anvil at the summons of war, let women now leave all that may be left of home for a great and earnest day of counsel. Let them meet first as women, to bewail and commemorate the dead. Let them solemnly take counsel with each other as the means whereby the great human family can live in peace, and each bearing after her own time the sacred impress, not of Caesar, but of God.

Julia Ward Howe [189]

We can never make the world safe for democracy by fighting...

Every nation must learn that all the people of the nations are children of God and must all share the wealth of the world. You may say this is impracticable, far away, and can never be accomplished. But this is the work which Universalists are appointed to do. Universalists sometimes, somehow, somewhere, must ever teach this great lesson.

Olympia Brown [190]

All human beings have the propensity for good and evil, for violence and non-violence. This is an inheritance from evolution, from the animals from which we developed, and from the struggle for survival, but unlike our animal ancestors, we have an awareness that allows us to see the consequences of our actions and to make moral choices.

All the great religions exalt compassion, forgiveness, reconciliation in personal relationships. When it comes to group relationships, however, these virtues struggle to be recognised as such – there is a dualism, one standard for the interpersonal, another for the collective, especially so with violence...

The trouble is that it is often taken for granted that no alternative is available. But that is not true. In fact non-violent forms of action for political ends have for long been in use. Here are a few techniques: strikes, boycotts, sit-ins, vigils, marches, non-cooperation, and civil disobedience – about which Thoreau wrote a classic. These and others can be used as a substitute for taking up arms. Gandhi and Martin Luther King were masters of these methods, but their use is in fact much more widespread than generally realised. Norwegian teachers during the Nazi occupation, shipyard workers in Poland in 1980, school students in apartheid South Africa are some who have demonstrated its effectiveness.

Not only do human beings – in a world of literally genocidal weapons – need to give up their faith in the effectiveness of armed force, but the ethically, and even practically, superior method of active non-violence is available to all.

George Paxton [191]

I accept, as one of the basic ethical principles, the principle of the minimization of the amount of suffering in the world...

I cannot in good faith argue that I deserve a better fate than other men; and I am forced by this logic to accept as the fundamental ethical principle the Golden Rule: "As ye would that men should do to you, do ye also to them likewise" (Luke [6:31])...

We suffer from accidents, from natural catastrophes, from disease, from the ills accompanying the deterioration of age, and also, in a sense the most viciously, from man's inhumanity to man, as expressed in economic exploitation, the maldistribution of the world's wealth, and especially the evil institution of war...

There is great misery caused by the abject poverty of about half of the world's people; yet most of the scientists and technologists of the world today are working to make the rich richer and the poor poorer, or are working on the development and fabrication of terrible engines of mass destruction and death, whose use might end our civilization and exterminate the human race...

I believe that it is a violation of the natural law for half of the people of the world to live in misery, in abject poverty, without hope for the future, while the affluent nations spend on militarism a sum of money equal to the entire income of this miserable half of the world's people...

The injustice and immorality of the great wars of the past would be far transcended by a great war in the nuclear age, a war in which the devastating weapons involving nuclear fission and fusion that now exist were used. Instead of tens of millions, hundreds or even thousands of millions of human beings might be killed... There is even the possibility that the human race would not survive the catastrophes.

As rational and moral beings, we are forced now to find a rational and moral alternative to war.

Linus Pauling [192]

Part IV:
How to Live Unitarianly

The purpose of religious faith is not merely belief. The Unitarian faith, the Unitarian Life, is a practical religious way of life. To be a Unitarian is to live the Unitarian Life, to live "Unitarianly". What does this mean? It means that Unitarians live religious lives, always open to new knowledge, but guided by the wisdom of those who have gone before us.

Part IV offers guidance for this spiritual path that we walk. Here you will find the collective wisdom of Unitarians through the ages on themes such as living fully, openly, and honestly; living a life spiritually awake and aware; religious seeking and finding; spiritual growth; spiritual practice and prayer; facing all the challenges that life brings to our bodies and souls; dying; engaging in relationships; giving; and being committed to fighting evil and injustice in the world.

How to live Unitarianly

Faith is not an abstraction, but a way of living.

Palfrey Perkins [193]

Because Unitarianism imbues my whole life, it of necessity affects the way I practise medicine. As I believe in the value of every individual and can cope with pluralism, I usually try to avoid the traps of racism, ageism, and sexism. My ideas about the "after-life" do not interfere with my care of terminally ill patients. Thoughts about the unborn do not constrain me in counselling women seeking abortions. Our lack of dogma frees me to make my own decisions in matters of ethics. Above all, I aim to enable people to reach their own informed decisions by educating them about their own bodies and I try to give my disadvantaged patients a feeling of their own worth in a world which is for ever trying to devalue them; and as well as asking "Why?", I also ask "Why not?"

Jane Williams [194]

Social action must begin, not with grand motions at conferences, or token protests, but with the Buddhist notion of "right living". I need to address and re-address the question: "How can I be and do in the world, in a way that creates less harm and does more good?" In one of the twelve steps of the Alcoholics Anonymous process, recovering addicts are asked to write their inventory of the times when they have created harm and the times when they have created goodness, as a step towards acceptance of the truth, responsibility, repentance, and self-forgiveness. Not an easy task for any of us. In the Alcoholics Anonymous prayer, one prays for "the courage to change what I can change; the humility to accept what I cannot change; and the wisdom to know the difference".

Peter Hawkins [195]

If any light can pierce and scatter the clouds of prejudice, it is that of a pure example... may your life preach more loudly than your lips...

To all who hear me, I would say, with the Apostle, Prove all things, hold fast that which is good. Do not, brethren, shrink from the duty of searching God's Word for yourselves, through fear of human censure and denunciation. Do not think that you may innocently follow the opinions which prevail around you, without investigation.

William Ellery Channing [196]

God send us a real religious life, which shall pluck blindness out of the heart, and make us better fathers, mothers, and children! a religious life that shall go with us where we go, and make every home a house of God, every act acceptable as prayer. We would work for this, and pray for it, though we wept tears of blood while we prayed.

Theodore Parker [197]

Today well lived makes every tomorrow a sacrament of joy.

Robert Henry Holmes [198]

Life is a wonderful, precious thing,
Yet even in the most difficult circumstances,
Those times that stretch us beyond endurance,
When we wonder why,
There is a cruel beauty,
A lesson to be learnt.

Always there is something good just waiting to be discovered,
Some personal growth to be gained,
Some knowledge about ourselves to unfold,
Some spiritual understanding which excites our being.

To learn about love and understanding;
To love ourselves as others love us;
To bring the healing warmth of love to as many people as we can;
To spread love and understanding around us wherever we go, to
   people,
to our fellow creatures who share this world with us, and to the
   earth itself;
To learn to understand ourselves and to reach out to bring that
   spark of understanding to them.

To learn about giving and forgiving;
To give without expectation of any reward;
To receive as graciously and happily as we give;
To forgive ourselves and to teach others how to forgive;
To feel complete, content and loved, however much we receive;
To help others in many different, healing ways.

To learn about peace and harmony;
To feel at peace with ourselves;
To live in harmony with our environment;
To bring the experience of peace and contentment to ourselves and
   those around us;
To be gentle, and to spread that gentleness in a warm tide amongst
   those we meet,
To find peace, joy, happiness in everything we do, and are, and
   have been, and will be.

To discover the limitless nature of our being;
To open our eyes to the beauties and wonder of this world, and of
   the next;
To understand the vastness of eternity;
To realise that darkness is not emptiness;
To discover our own spiritual path;
To help others find their spiritual paths;
To be at one with All That Is;
To be at one.

Penny Quest [199]

Our life is frittered away by detail... Simplify!

Henry David Thoreau [200]

We need people like you – the Class X type who is not bothered about their own status in the world because they feel secure in themselves; who can walk with king and peasant alike without feeling inferior or superior; who is neither In crowd or Out crowd.

We need the company of the spiritual pilgrim who feels a sense of the greatness of all life and the universe in which we live; who feels there is a holiness which has direction and guides them to love and care for the world in which we live. Who call this holiness God or call it Angels or call it the Spirit of Life makes no difference. They are the pilgrims who can walk along the way and talk with their friends and discuss the way they feel – they listen and they value the opinion of their friends and they have their own opinions to share, but will not argue that their own view is best or that their friends must change.

We need the company of equals who will not discriminate against the opposite sex or against colour or creed or sexual orientation.

We have a vision of a world where everyone has the right to be educated and the right to be cured of illness and the right to work and the right to speak.

We need friends who will support us when we are confronted by a life crisis, and we need friends who will share our joys and our triumphs. Friends who enjoy life and company.

With our fellow pilgrims we meet together in friendship for worship – to give thanks for life; to be inspired through prayer and discourse on scriptures; to reach for that sense of holiness which is the centre of our lives.

Come and join the Unitarians.

Tony McNeile [201]

Living fully and deliberately

Give us the spirit of the child. Give us the child who lives within: the child who trusts, the child who imagines, the child who sings, the child who receives without reservation, the child who gives without judgment. Give us a child's eyes, that we may receive the beauty and the freshness of this day like a sunrise; give us a child's ears, that we may hear the music of mythical times; give us a child's heart, that we may be filled with wonder and delight; give us a child's faith, that we may be cured of our cynicism; give us the spirit of a child, who is not afraid to need; who is not afraid to love.

Sarah York [202]

Why should we live in such a hurry and waste of life? We are determined to be starved before we are hungry. I wish to live deliberately, to front only the essential facts of life. I wish to learn what life has to teach, and not, when I come to die, discover that I have not lived. I do not wish to live what is not life, living is so dear, nor do I wish to practice resignation, unless it is quite necessary. I wish to live deep and suck out all the marrow of life, I want to cut a broad swath, to drive life into a corner, and reduce it to its lowest terms. If it proves to be mean, then to get the whole and genuine meanness of it, and publish its meanness to the world; or if it is sublime, to know it by experience, and to be able to give a true account of it.

Henry David Thoreau [203]

The spiritual traditions tell us that we can learn to correct our vision and that, in one sense, it is very simple to do: we have to start by looking at things. But, you may protest, I look at things all the time. No you don't. You no more see with your eyes than you hear with your ears or you communicate with your speech. For most of your life you are a passive receiver of visual impressions, which is not nearly the same as being an attentive observer. In our somnambulism we rarely actually look at anything or listen to anything. This is why we constantly forget things. "Where are my keys?" "Where are my glasses?" "Where's my wallet?" We misplace things, or forget them every day, because we live distractedly, inadvertently, even making a virtue out of our forgetfulness by imagining that it shows our unconcern with the mundane and trivial aspects of our existence – my mind is in higher realms, we fool ourselves into thinking. "I can never remember people's names," says a friend of mine. The reason he can never remember them is because he never learned them in the first place. When the name was announced to him, he was too busy thinking about the impression he was making on this new person that he never even momentarily paid any attention to the name. How guilty are we all of this and similar inadvertence? "To be awake is to be alive," writes Thoreau in *Walden*. "I have never yet met a man who was quite awake. How could I have looked him in the face?"

Bill Darlison [204]

Facing truth and speaking truth

We often give to others advice we need ourselves.

Roy D. Phillips [205]

Whatever you may suffer, speak the truth. Be worthy of the entire confidence of your associates. Consider what is right as what must be done. It is not necessary that you should keep your property, or even your life, but it is necessary that you should hold fast your integrity.

William Ellery Channing [206]

In addition to seeking truth and finding truth, there is facing truth. An unremitting readiness to confront the facts can prove unsettling. There are truths we would rather ignore: truth about ourselves, our inherited assumptions, our backgrounds, our partners, even our cherished ideologies. But the mission of Unitarian Universalism remains to come together and, fortified by the nudges and embraces of our companions, to stand tall and face whatever harsh truths existence delivers.

There is more. Speaking the truth is also an imperative for freethinkers. Telling the truth is more complicated than either lying or remaining silent. We belong to a legacy of prophets who assailed the social and theological orthodoxies of their day.

Tom Owen-Towle [207]

Whom God enlightened by His spirit must not be silent and must not hide the truth.

Francis David [208]

Living in the present

These roses under my window make no reference to former roses or to better ones; they are for what they are; they exist with God today. There is no time to them. There is simply the rose; it is perfect in every moment of its existence. Before a leaf-bud has burst, its whole life acts; in the full-blown flower there is no more, in the leafless root there is no less. Its nature is satisfied, and it satisfies nature in all moments alike.

But we postpone or remember. We do not live in the present, but with reverted eye lament the past, or, heedless of the riches that surround us, stand on tiptoe to foresee the future. We cannot be happy or strong until we too live with nature in the present, above time.

Ralph Waldo Emerson (adapted) [209]

Whatever the destiny of the planet or of the individual life, a sustaining meaning is discernable and commanding in the here and now. Anyone who denies this denies that there is anything worth taking seriously or even worth talking about. Every blade of grass, every work of art, every scientific endeavor, every striving for righteousness bears witness to this meaning. Indeed, every frustration or perversion of truth, beauty or goodness also bears witness, as the shadow points round to the sun.

James Luther Adams [210]

There is a well-known story concerning Rabbi Zusya, in which he addresses his congregation just before his own death: "In the world to come they will not ask me, 'Why were you not more like Moses?' They will ask me, 'Why were you not more like Zusya?'"

In our liberal religious communities we stress the vital insight of this story by encouraging people to *"come as you are"*. This is another way of saying that we accept the challenge to seek the truth about ourselves, and our world (one inescapable context of our being). It is a challenge to live *mindfully*: the practice of living fully in the moment, or the "eternal now". Yet, in part, true mindfulness can be brought about only by dispelling illusions – and some of the most compelling illusions are those that we inherit from the past. The Unitarian movement's traditional dedication to sound historical scholarship is the chief way in which we have sought to uncover the truth about the past, in order that we may live ever more in the moment, free from illusions, but still open to the many eternal truths which history has preserved for us.

Andrew Brown [211]

Courage

This is not a time for liberals of the genteel tradition who are frightened in the presence of explosive issues that blast their world and shake the earth. It is not a time for liberals of the pious tradition who believe that all is right with the world and that all things work together for good. It is not a time for confused liberals who move simultaneously in all directions without arriving anywhere in particular.

This is a time for liberals who believe that the only form of society worth building and perpetuating is one grounded in respect for the integrity of persons, committed to critical inquiry and devoted to abundant freedom.

Curtis Reese [212]

Courage is the indispensable substance of religious liberalism. It makes "the spirit live' when "the word killeth". It takes courage not to settle for a religion "once for all delivered to the Saints". It requires courage to be unwilling to accept the proposition that God, having spoken at some time remote in antiquity, is now aloof and distant, as though one were dead, as though religion were merely an antiquarian interest. The religious liberal accepts the proposition and responds to the challenge that religion is a universal expression of the human spirit which everywhere seeks to break forth in new, fresh expressions.

George N. Marshall [213]

Making decisions

My friend Joe taught in Ghana back in the sixties, where he translated into English six folk tales of the native Ashanti people. Each is a sort of a wry parable with its moral expressed in an aphorism of the sort the Ashanti use to speak of weighty matters. For example,

If the tree is to flourish, the branches must flourish.

In one, a struggling tinker is helped by his family to become a prosperous trader. They lend him money and give him good advice. After all, they reflect, *If the tree is to flourish, the branches must flourish.*

And he does indeed prosper. Yet he is not happy. Asking advice of the local sage, he is offered another agrarian motto:

If the yam does not flourish, it is due to the soil.

The message is clear.

There was only one explanation for such a simple truth. The soil in which Kwabeba's new life was planted was unsuitable. If you have been born with the soul of a tinker, you cannot change your soul by changing your trade.

How wise are the Ashanti! They know something that our own materialistic society too often overlooks: that the work you choose must suit your soul.

Our society teaches other ways to choose a career: assess your needs and abilities and find a suitable vehicle for them, considering security and prospects. But true suitability must fit body, mind, *and* spirit; and we are not often taught to take note of the third. Luckily, some of us stumble on work that suits the soul too.

No, it's more than stumbling. Some of us, blessed in our freedom to choose, catch sound of the still small voice and respond to its song. And it's more than luck – inner listening is something we can practise ourselves and teach our children.

"The Tinker" is a simple tale; life need not be all-or-nothing. Not all of us can make soul work our life's work, but we can and should all do something in our lives that makes our souls sing. We know it when we find it, because then we are fully alive.

What makes your soul sing?

Joy Croft [214]

Each new morning two choices are open to every one of us:
The choice to live that day in the joyfulness of Love,
Or in the darkness of Fear.

Each new day, as the sun rises,
We have another opportunity to make that choice.
The symbolism of the sunrise is the removal of shadow
And the return of Light.

Each new morning we have another chance
To rid ourselves of the burdens, sorrows and fears of the past,
To rejoice in the joy of the present,
And to look forward to a future of fulfillment
On every level of our being.

Each sunrise is a fresh opportunity to release fear,
To choose a different life-path,
To commit ourselves to joyful, light living,
To trust in Ourselves and in the Universe,
To trust in the forces of Nature and in Mother Earth,
To trust in God, the Creator, the All-That-Is.

Penny Quest [215]

I am often called upon to counsel individuals who feel trapped in painful impasses of indecision. Intellectually, even emotionally, they seem ready to execute a breakthrough and forge in a new direction. But they keep demurring: "I can't do it. I can't do it." To which I invariably say: "I believe you may not be ready to make the change. I even believe that perhaps you won't ever do it. But I will not agree that you *can't* do it. The *can'ts* in your life are few, and this isn't one of them!"

We humans crave autonomy, yet dread it. We fear, then avoid making decisions. To determine our futures is at last to run the risk of falling or failing. These multiple fears are captured in the English phrase: "To take the plunge". Yet taking the plunge as card-carrying heretics is exactly what the religious course of Unitarian Universalism demands.

Tom Owen-Towle [216]

Questions, answers, and religious seeking

From an early age I found it difficult to get satisfying answers to my many religious questions. I am still trying to find answers, but I now realize that there is no specific religious persuasion to furnish me with answers. I must look within myself for the knowledge that satisfies my quest. Being a Unitarian Universalist, I don't feel stigmatized for asking questions. I enjoy the camaraderie of exchanging ideas and concepts with fellow Unitarian Universalists. My search for truth continues. It's more enjoyable, however, to be associated with others who are also seeking their own individual truths and answers.

James A. Robinson [217]

Unanswered questions are far less dangerous than unquestioned answers.

Anonymous [218]

We receive fragments of holiness, glimpses of eternity, brief moments of insight. Let us gather them up for the precious gifts that they are and, renewed by their grace, move boldly into the unknown.

Sarah York [219]

You must lay aside all prejudices on both sides, and neither believe nor reject anything because any other persons, or description of persons, have rejected or believed it. Your own reason is the only oracle given you by heaven, and you are answerable, not for the rightness, but the uprightness of the decision.

Thomas Jefferson [220]

I know that in faith and with your whole heart you question me. Therefore I am glad because of you. Truly I say to you I am pleased, and my Father in me rejoices, that thus you inquire and ask. Your boldness makes me rejoice, and it affords yourself life.

Jesus of Nazareth [221]

Belief and doubt

It matters what we believe. Some beliefs are like walled gardens. They encourage exclusiveness and feelings of being especially privileged. Other beliefs are expansive and lead the way into wider and deeper sympathies.

Some beliefs are like shadows, clouding children's days with fears of unknown calamities. Other beliefs are like sunshine, blessing children with the warmth of happiness.

Some beliefs are divisive, separating the saved from the unsaved, friends and enemies. Other beliefs are bonds in a world community, where sincere differences beautify the pattern.

Some beliefs are like blinders, shutting off the power to choose one's own direction. Other beliefs are like gateways opening wide vistas for exploration.

Some beliefs weaken a person's selfhood. They blight the growth of resourcefulness. Other beliefs nurture self-confidence and enrich the feeling of personal worth.

Some beliefs are rigid, like the body of death, impotent in a changing world. Other beliefs are pliable, like the young sapling, ever growing with the upward thrust of life.

Sophia Lyon Fahs [222]

Believe nothing because a wise man said it.
Believe nothing because it is generally held.
Believe nothing because it is written.
Believe nothing because it is said to be divine.
Believe nothing because someone else believes it.
But believe only what you yourself judge to be true.

The Buddha [223]

The weakest faith is that which fears doubt.

J. Frank Schulman [224]

Cherish your doubts, for doubt is the attendant of truth. Doubt is the key to the door of knowledge; it is the servant of discovery. A belief that may not be questioned binds us to error, for there is incompleteness and imperfection in every belief. Doubt is the touchstone of truth; it is an acid which eats away the false. Let no one fear for the truth, that doubt may consume it; for doubt is a testing of belief.

The truth stands boldly and unafraid; it is not shaken by the testing: for truth, if it be truth, arises from each testing stronger, more secure. Those that would silence doubt are filled with fear; their houses are built on shifting sands. But those who fear not doubt, and know its use, are founded on rock. They shall walk in the light of growing knowledge; the work of their hands shall endure.

Therefore let us not fear doubt, but let us rejoice in its help: it is to the wise as a staff to the blind; doubt is the attendant of truth.

Robert T. Weston [225]

It is necessary to the happiness of man that he be mentally faithful to himself. Infidelity does not consist in believing or in disbelieving; it consists in professing to believe what he does not believe.

It is impossible to calculate the moral mischief, if I may so express it, that mental lying has produced in society. When a man has so far corrupted and prostituted the chastity of his mind as to subscribe to his professional belief to things he does not believe, he has prepared himself for the commission of every other crime.

Thomas Paine [226]

There can be no reliable faith for the free unless there are faith-ful men and women who form the faith into beliefs, who test and criticize the beliefs, and who then transform and transmit the beliefs. This process of forming and transforming the beliefs of the free faith is a process of discussion; it is a co-operative endeavor in which people surrender to the commanding, transforming reality. The only way men and women can reliably form and transform beliefs is through the sharing of tradition and new insights, and through the co-operative criticism and testing of tradition and insight. In other words, people must sincerely work with each other in order to give reliable form and expression to faith. This is the only way freedom *from* tyranny can be fulfilled in freedom *with* justice and truth.

James Luther Adams [227]

Many of us religious liberals have not given sufficient thought to what we believe. We recite no dogmatic creed. We have no finished faith, once revealed and now neatly packaged and sealed.

Are we in danger then of going to the opposite extreme – of being hopelessly vague about what we believe?

Perhaps we should realize that our need is not to "find something to believe" – but rather to discover what our lives indicate that we believe right now. This is the place to start.

What did we enjoy most in the day just past? How did we spend our time? How do we wish we might have spent it? How do we feel about ourselves at the end of the day? Do we like the kind of person we are? What do we worry about? What are we afraid of? What do we hope for? Whose lives did our lives touch during the day? Was it for better or worse? How do we feel about our parents, spouse, children, neighbors, the school, the town? Are we aware of the natural universe? Do the arts influence us and feed our spirits?

To bring our attitudes, our convictions, our practices, out into the open and to look at them systematically is to find out what we actually believe.

Edith Hunter [228]

Salvation and spiritual growth

The salvationist faith is a faith that cannot save us. There could easily be more revivalist services when the hydrogen bombs were falling than ever before in history. The faith that can save us is a faith that does affect our entire lives – both individual and national. It is not a faith that calls upon God to do what God will never do; it calls upon the Godlike in ourselves – yes, and it asks for endless courage and unwearying endeavor.

A. Powell Davies [229]

The aim of religion is not to get us into Heaven, but to get Heaven into us.

Ulysses G. B. Pierce [230]

What we are is God's gift to us. What we become is our gift to God.

Ralph Waldo Emerson [231]

In the past, our movement had influence out of all proportion to its size; but at present, like many other denominations, we seem to have lost our path, and have failed to identify the unique contribution that a liberal religious approach could offer. Could it be that there is a new work to do, and that through our courses in religious education, our worship, and other activities we could be promoting the development of spiritual intelligence, thereby making a difference to our society once more?

Sarah Tinker [232]

A spiritually growing person – like a spiritually growing congregation – is developing awareness and a capacity to pay attention to what is at hand in daily tasks and encounters, as a template for understanding and filling a place in the wider scheme of things. This is an empowering vision for congregational practice.

Michaela von Britzke [233]

The old man, the man of the first creation, becomes new only gradually, step-by-step over time, partially due to God's grace and partially from his/her own efforts. The animal-like man, the old Adam, the man of rough instincts becomes sanctified just as Abraham did, that is, arrives at a higher value stage of evolution.

Francis David [234]

I have never agreed with those who tried to tell us that the whole idea of sin is out of date. To the best of my observation and belief, sin is highly contemporary, and we are all up to our necks in it.

But that doesn't mean that to avoid drowning in sin we must clutch at theological straws. It doesn't mean that we must surrender all attempts at swimming our way to shore. Nor does it mean that there is nothing else to do but call on God for a miracle...

If the world is saved – it seems to me – it will be saved by those who bring to God their sweat and toil, not by those who have nothing to bring but their tears.

A. Powell Davies [235]

God does not expect you to save the world. Your mandate is limited to one single human being, which may be just yourself – or your neighbour. God never expects more from us than we are capable of doing. Each word of comfort, each act of compassion, is a small bonfire in the thundering nights. But these tiny flickering flames, the simple gestures of loving hearts, will add up and will eventually save the world. Salvation is not something we have to wait for, but we must do something about. Because we can. Because we can, therefore we must.

Imre Gellérd [236]

Unitarians identify the agent of salvation as healing, dynamic love. This is both channelled through others and derived from some wellspring within ourselves. It is love that brings wholeness and fulfilment through the dissolution of the barriers that divide us. These barriers exist both inwardly and in the external world. The ultimate saviour is the source of love's power – which most call God.

However, love becomes manifest only in human beings and their relationships. So all those people who bring mercy and reconciliation, liberty and justice into the world are the embodiments of salvation. They are the "saviours" within humanity.

Cliff Reed [237]

Unitarian spirituality

There is a continuous relationship between religious experience and all other experience. This we need to remember.

George N. Marshall [238]

In every life there are certain moments which partake of another, higher order of experience – peculiarly precious moments which offer serenity, hope, and strength and which allow us to return to the demands of daily life with renewed vitality and confidence. The growth of a spiritual dimension in each of us as individuals seems to result in a multiplication and a deepening of such moments both in ourselves and in the world.

Elizabeth M. Jones [239]

Let us learn the revelation of all nature and thought: that the Highest dwells within us, that the sources of nature are in our own minds. As there is no screen or ceiling between our heads and the infinite heavens, so there is no bar or wall in the soul where we, the effect, cease, and God, the cause, begins.

I am constrained every moment to acknowledge a higher origin for events than the will I call mine. There is a deep power in which we exist and whose beatitude is accessible to us. Every moment when the individual feels invaded by it is memorable. It comes to the lowly and simple; it comes to whosoever will put off what is foreign and proud; it comes as insight; it comes as serenity and grandeur. The soul's health consists in the fullness of its reception. For ever and ever the influx of this better and more universal self is new and unsearchable.

Within us is the soul of the whole; the wise silence, the universal beauty, to which every part and particle is equally related; the eternal One. When it breaks through our intellect, it is genius; when it breathes through our will, it is virtue; when it flows through our affections, it is love.

Ralph Waldo Emerson [240]

Our spirit dwelling in us is God his very self; and that this is the Holy Spirit in us, according to the saying of the prophet, is shown by the Apostle, saying, "The Spirit of God in us", because God said, "I will dwell in them."... And herein we bear witness to a certain heavenly feeling, and a hidden divine something, for when it bloweth where it will, I hear the voice thereof, but know not whence it cometh, or whither it goeth...

Hence I always say that the Holy Spirit is the activity of God in the spirit of man.

Michael Servetus [241]

Every spiritual experience is in its essential nature a mystery; every yearning after things Divine, every prayer sent up to the Infinite, every aspiration after eternity... We can only understand the Divine language if we attune our minds to it; only by looking for the essence and reality of things shall we become aware that there is a Divine Reality in all things.

Gertrude von Petzold [242]

Here then it is that there is room for true communion, – that Spirit may meet Spirit, and that the sacred silence may itself speak the exchange of love. Our moral ideals, the irrepressible sigh after higher perfection, the sense of Divine authority in every vision of the better, the shame at every yielding to the worse, these, we are well aware, are not of our making, or donations of other men; they are above us; they are given to us; they are what draw us to God, and commence our likeness to him. In this field of spiritual affection that lies around our will, the common essence of man and God, the divine element that spreads its margins into us, has its home, its life, its reciprocal recognition; its bursts of human prayer, its answer of Divine compassion; its deep shadows of contrition, and returning gleams of restoration. The life with God then, of which saintly men in every age have testified, is no illusion of enthusiasm, but an ascent, through simple surrender, to the higher vision of the soul, the very watchtower whence there is the clearest and largest view. The bridge is thus complete between the Divine and the human personality; and we crown the religion of Causation, the religion of Conscience, by the religion of the Spirit.

James Martineau [243]

I went out one afternoon for a walk alone. I was in the empty unthinking state in which one saunters along country lanes, simply yielding oneself to the casual sights around, which give a town-bred lad with country yearning such intense delight. Suddenly I became conscious of the presence of someone else.

I cannot describe it, but I felt that I had as direct perception of the being of God all round about me as I have of you when we are together. It was no longer a matter of inference, it was an immediate act of spiritual (or whatever adjective you like to employ) apprehension. It came unsought, absolutely unexpectedly.

I remember the wonderful transfiguration of the far-off woods and hills as they seemed to blend in the infinite being with which I was thus brought into relation. This experience did not last long. But it sufficed to change all my feeling. I had not found God, because I had never looked for him. But he had found me.

Joseph Estlin Carpenter [244]

A number of researchers have investigated aspects of spirituality and have concluded that the capacity for spiritual experience is biologically natural to all human beings, and that it is more evident within children than in adults. Many of us have experienced the piercing nature of children's questions ("but *why* is it like that?"), and we know that our young people's questions have a freshness which we cynical adults sometimes lack.

Sarah Tinker [245]

What is it within us which wells up when we need it most?
That God-sense which is always there;
That inspiration which appears out of nowhere;
That faith in ourselves which takes us by surprise;
That moment of understanding which enables us to call upon our
    reserves
To try again.

We all have within us those fundamental resources of love and joy;
A sense of humour which can turn the most dire happening
Into reason for laughter;
Inner strength which can be called upon
When we come to the aid of others or when we need help
    ourselves;
Inner wisdom which provides the answers to our unspoken
    questions.

There is never a moment when we are alone;
Never a moment when our cries for help will not be answered;
Never a moment when we are left unsupported;
Never a moment when insight is not available to us;
Never a moment when we are not connected to God, the Universe,
    and All-That-Is.

Penny Quest [246]

Prayer, meditation, and contemplation

A medieval monk by the name of Theophilus noted that prayer was talking to God, and meditation was listening to God. Unitarian Universalists do too much talking it often seems, among themselves, but the art of meditation, of listening is an essential virtue and necessity. Indeed, many of our churches have periods of meditations rather than prayers in service. In an age that puts great stress on communication, the form of communication called prayer should call for attention. It is the direct means by which we relate ourselves through directed thought with a cause and relationship larger than our human fellowship, and it is very important.

George N. Marshall [247]

I love the silent church before the service better than all the preaching.

Ralph Waldo Emerson [248]

Shortly before he died, the Buddha said to his followers: "Be you lamps unto yourselves; be your own reliance. Hold to the truth within yourselves, as to the only lamp."

Centuries later, the poet Robert Browning wrote: "Truth is within ourselves, it takes no rise from outward things, whate'er you may believe. There is an inmost centre in us all, where truth abides in fullness..."

Unitarians have similarly emphasised the primacy of inner truth over external authority, and the importance of discovering it for ourselves, so that we can relate to the world authentically with enlightened reason and conscience.

The various spiritual traditions teach a range of meditational practices for discovering the truth within ourselves. In the Christian tradition, for example, there is contemplative prayer, and in Buddhism *vipassana* (insight meditation), and there are similar practices taught by Sufis, Hindu yogis, Taoists, and shamans, each prescribing methods for undertaking a psychological journey through the layers of the human psyche to the "inmost centre".

Spiritual guides emphasise the need for sustained courage and faith in those who undertake this journey of self-exploration, for it is a difficult path through the Dark Nights of the soul, in which the person discovers disturbing tendencies and inclinations arising from deep, unconscious roots of ego-attachment. But commitment to the process of self-inquiry brings rewards. As fearful attachments to the ego are progressively dissolved, there is a growing sense of freedom to live and love and relate to the world in a new way.

A deep truth about our humanity comes more clearly to consciousness as the inquiry continues, that beyond the suffering of ego-loss are the eternal springs of Wisdom and Love at the inmost centre – that God, the Tao, Buddhahood, Brahman (whatever cultural form we choose to point to it) is the source and ground of our humanity, and that this is the Life that will freely flow through us when the "self" has been surrendered. Meditation is the practice of progressively peeling off layers of ego so that who I truly am can come to fullness.

David Monk [249]

God listens to the heart, not to words.

Gaston M. Carrier [250]

Prayer does not change things; prayer changes people, and people change things.

Lon Ray Call [251]

I try to pray.
I want to pray.
I need to pray
For support – for help – for reassurance
But the words won't come.
I can't find suitable words.
I know in my heart what I am feeling
And – maybe – those feelings are a prayer in themselves.
But that is not enough for me.
Until I have expressed what is worrying me.
(Spoken the words out loud
Said what is in my heart
Given voice to anxieties
Which haunt me
Which fill me with fear
Which surround me
Like a cloak which is too warm on a Summer day
Or too thin in an icy wind).
Until I can find those words
I remain ill at ease.
My inability to pray my prayer
Just adds to my worry.
I try to empty my mind
I try to see – in my mind's eye –
A pale blue cloudless sky
A silent landscape
Untouched by noise or movement
And then ....

My prayer is simple ....

Help me to pray
Put the words in my mouth.
Help me to say what is in my heart
Take away my fear of saying it.
Just – help me to say ....
Just – help me to pray!

Stephanie Ramage [252]

Many people have discarded prayer because they think that prayer must be petitionary, which they regard – I think correctly – as childish. But the prayers of the saints rose beyond this. They called it meditation, and, a further stage, contemplation. For ourselves, we may wish to call it inner discourse, or reflection at the highest level of which we are capable. It is rash indeed to be disdainful of this discipline. Day after day, we look at life through petty hopes and fear, and often through our prejudices. Should there not be a time, each day, for looking at it from a higher level? To me, the best time is the end of the day, and that might be the time, I think, for many people. To look back over the day and judge it – judge it, first of all, severely. The things we said, the truths we didn't speak, the wasted moments of resentment or of foolish pride. The fears we did not cast out, the fretful aims that possessed us – the same aims that have always disappointed us. Let these and all else that need it be severely judged.

And then, let us see what there was of good in the day, and how we could have kept on friendlier terms not only with the world but with ourselves. Whether we turn this thinking towards God or just meditate in our own hearts, this is prayer, and the power of God is in it. There is a sort of duality in each of us, a discussion within our innermost thoughts. The nobler voice will be said by some of us – myself, for instance – to be the voice of God. Not literally, of course, but in source and spiritual vitality. Others of us will call it our better nature. But no matter what it be called, its presence is a firm reality. We cultivate our inner lives, and thereby raise the quality of all our living, by giving definite times to such discipline. And to the extent that we see the world more clearly and ourselves and our part in it more plainly, we gain wisdom and sureness of direction; and this, in turn, relieves the tension that the world imposes on us – much of which is due to vacillation and uncertainty – and brings us closer to serenity.

A. Powell Davies [253]

My son Billy, then fifteen years old, had overdosed on drugs, and it was unclear whether he would live. As I sat with him in the hospital, I found myself praying. First the selfish prayers for forgiveness . . . for the time not made, for the too many trips, for the many things unsaid, and, sadly, for a few things said that should never had passed my lips. But as the night darkened, I finally found the pure prayer. The prayer that asked only that my son would live. And late in the evening, I felt the hands of a loving universe reaching out – the hands of God, the Spirit of Life. The name was unimportant. I knew that those hands would be there to hold me whatever the morning brought. And I knew, though I cannot tell you how, that those hands were holding my son as well. I knew that I did not have to walk that path alone, that there is a love that has never broken faith with us and never will.

William G. Sinkford [254]

Happiness

Happiness is the only good. The time to be happy is now. The place to be happy is here. The way to be happy is to make others so. This creed is somewhat short, but it is long enough for this life; long enough for this world. If there is another world, when we get there we can make another creed. But this creed will certainly do for this life.

Robert G. Ingersoll [255]

In the attic of my home in Maine, I once discovered a yellowed letter written by a man in response to the death of a relative. "She died happy. She was a Universalist." Dying happy is not one of my life goals, but I was reminded of an empowering lesson I had learned in my Universalist church school. It is best expressed by the poet Milton: "The mind is its own place and in itself can make a Hell of Heaven, a Heaven of Hell." Universalism is a matter of spirit more than a theology. It is generous spirit searching for the good in all things and expecting the best from others and oneself. I can live happily with that!

Drusilla Cummins [256]

My happiness will be incomplete while one creature remains miserable.

George de Benneville [257]

All joys and tears alike are sent to give the soul fit nourishment.

Sarah Flower Adams [258]

We believe that holiness and true happiness are inseparably connected.

The Universalist Winchester Profession of Faith (1803) [259]

Above all, it would be desirable to separate from religion that idea of gloom, which in this country has but too generally accompanied it.

Anna Laetitia Aikin Barbauld [260]

I believe that laughter is life's saving grace. As George Bernard Shaw reminds us: "We need ever-deeper wisdom and ever-broader compassion; laughter lubricates the job." Without humor we are joyless crusaders. We must also negotiate the fine line being serious and being grim.

Tom Owen-Towle [261]

Life journeys

I was born and raised in a National Baptist Convention church. At age three, I felt called to the ministry, but by age ten I experienced doubts about the nature of God and the purpose of humankind. I was active in the church and always asking questions. By age fifteen, I had been tried for heresy and convicted of sin, and the right hand of fellowship had been withdrawn. It was then that I joined the Universalist Church. With the Universalist Church of America's ecclesiastical endorsement, I entered college and then theological school – a discontented theist with growing deistic leanings.

After completing theological school, I served a rural Universalist congregation part-time for three years, worked as a prison chaplain for seven years, worked with a Unitarian Universalist city mission agency for ten years, and am now serving as an interim minister. Religion is important to me as a way to understand existence. Humans exist to experience life, and I am unsure and unaware of any ultimate purpose or design. I want to enjoy life in the here and now, and the UU church is a place where I can, with self-respect and dignity, while exercising freedom and responsibility.

Thomas Payne [262]

Being a young person and being committed to anything even vaguely related to the word 'religious' is hard work these days.

I am 25, female, in stable and fulfilling paid work and also in a firm relationship with my partner Mick, who is also 25 but not a Unitarian. I was born into a strongly Unitarian family. My parents met through a British Unitarian organisation, my grandparents through an international one. One Grandfather was a Unitarian minister, the other a noted layperson. You may say, therefore, there was little question that I too would automatically feel at home in the Unitarian denomination, but it is never as simple as that.

I remember as a child an experience that perhaps started me off on the road to nonconformity. At a very early school assembly when I was aged about four and a half (when there were school places for the under fives), my Headmistress, whom I revered absolutely, told us the story of Noah and his Ark. I remember the isolation and terror I felt as I sat there thinking to myself "nobody could possibly build a boat big enough for two of every kind of animal in the world". Perhaps it was at that point that I became a Unitarian.

As a teenager I had another experience as I struggled to get to grips with my spiritual self. I was a member of a local Christian youth organisation that my best friend had introduced me to. After a worship service we divided into groups, and our group was led by a young woman who can hardly have been more than 18. One Sunday she described to us how she'd given up her boyfriend for Jesus. I was appalled at this notion, stunned that a religion could become so controlling. Ultimately I left the group.

I was fortunate enough to participate fully in innumerable Unitarian youth events as a teenager, which gave me the courage and tenacity to make my assault on the adult world. I was also fortunate enough to be part of a thriving local Sunday School as a younger child, an experience which definitely helped me to acquire an enquiring, if not always judicious, mind.

So, you ask, what does Unitarianism give me as a woman of today? Well, it gives me space and time to breathe, think and grow. It gives me access to broad-minded women and men, both young and old, who share in my quest to become a more rounded, fulfilled, living human being.

Helen Mason [263]

I wasn't actually born a Unitarian but, as I have always been inclined to question everything, I think I was one by inclination. So when as a young medical student I found my way to a Non-Subscribing Presbyterian Church (a denomination in Ireland historically linked with Unitarianism) in Belfast, I felt that I had found my spiritual home.

And what did I find? A feeling of worth as a human being and especially as a woman – and I think it was not just coincidence that the minister's wife was also a doctor. I found a spirit of enquiry into the scriptures, not only from traditional Christian sources but also from the other great religions of the world, and from secular sources. I learnt about the Ministry of all believers – a very novel idea for me, and a great contrast with the Anglicanism of my upbringing. I learnt about Reverence for Life, which overturned my idea that "Man should have dominion over animals". But the most revolutionary concept was that of working out our own theology, based on the scientific method which I was already absorbing in medical school.

Jane Williams [264]

Growing old

Each stage of individual development offers unique experience and opportunity. Certain experiences are possible only in youth – for example, the sense of the wide-openness of the future. There comes a time, however, when the individual may say, "Nevermore." Certain options – for example, career options – may no longer be open. Simone de Beauvoir at the age of fifty catalogs the things she will never do again: lie in the hay, slide on morning snow, win a first lover. But other experiences are possible only in fruited old age: the contemplation of satisfactions and beauties of long ago, the cherishing of *old* friendships, the exploration of opportunities previously unheeded (partly because of other importunate obligations), and also the meeting of the adversity of ill health (or of waning powers) with serenity and dignity. In conjugal relationships the love of the couple for each in middle life or in old age can possess unique qualities. To appreciate this uniqueness is something that requires thought and new sensitivity. A theology of ageing asserts, then, that each age group (and each person) has its own inimitable rendezvous with the coy mistress, the meaning of life.

James Luther Adams [265]

When we have a purpose to our living, we have a goal which can move us through any developmental stage...

People who have defined meaning to their life – detached from a physical or mental state – are able to accept change and maintain quality in their lives regardless of their circumstances. Aging well is about maturing the core of one's being from the external forms of affirmation that can be the focus of youth.

Aging is our best opportunity to integrate our life's experience into a grand and unique expression of our accumulated wisdom. When the changes of aging begin to appear and we realize that we are entering the last developmental moments, we have several choices – to rage against the dark night – to accept or deny, avoid or negotiate – to live in fear or faith. We choose. We decide how to frame what is given to us in the process of aging. We do not have to frame change as decline. We can choose to hold on to quality in our living and our loving as long as our minds are our own. Whether we remain standing, or are wheeling about in a chair or even flat out in bed – we can live in a creative and non-destructive way. We can either be pleasant and cheerful or growl, complain, and criticize. If not strong in body, we can remain strong in mind and spirit.

To age well we need to shift the core of our lives from the external to the internal. We must cultivate the centrality of hope, faith and love, deepening our sense of meaning in life through forgiveness, gratitude and joy.

Elaine Beth Peresluha [266]

Sickness, health, and healing

Well-being and being well are not always the same thing. I think we all understand that some people struggle with health issues all their life, and that out of that struggle, they create a very strong and vibrant theology that takes them through the rough times...

Current research shows over and over again... that our minds and our bodies are profoundly interdependent. It seems that taking good care of yourself means also developing healthy habits of mind, of mental and emotional health...

If you really sit down and just read the Gospels for yourself – what you see over and over again is Jesus is engaged in a relationship of healing *with people*. And it's not like the Evangelicals say where he's "zapping" people and they go knocking back, "Lord, I'm healed." It's never about that. It's about the establishment of relationship, out of which then healing can happen. It's the same for you and it's the same for me. In the end it's about being open to the forces that *can* heal us. We're not talking about cure; we're talking about healing, which is a much higher and more subtle definition. You and I may never be healed in any one specific place, but in our relationships and in our sense of being whole we can touch healing. And healing can certainly fill us over and over again. We can be love-filled. We can challenge, and we can comfort at the same time. That's the sense of wholeness...

Health is at last not the absence of sickness, but the sense of inner aliveness, of energy, and the ability to love, no matter what. In every dimension of our life. There's the old story of the man who goes into the doctor and says, "I don't know what's wrong with me. I hurt all over. If I touch my shoulder here it hurts. And if I touch my leg here it hurts. And if I touch my head here it hurts, and if I touch my foot it hurts. Doc, what's wrong?" The doctor says, "I think you've broken your finger." When it hurts like that, it's because of *what you're feeling with*.

Stephen Kendrick [267]

The body and the mind are so inseparably blended in the human constitution that we cannot deal with one portion of this compound nature without in more or less degree affecting the other. Our ministrations to body and soul cannot be separated by a sharply defined line. The arbitrary distinction between the physician of the body and the physician of the soul – doctor and priest – tends to disappear as science advances.

Elizabeth Blackwell [268]

Death, dying, and bereavement

Unitarians hold a wide variety of beliefs on this subject. Some have a very firm belief in personal survival beyond death, and cite evidence to support it.

Others – probably most – are less categorical, perhaps believing that in some way all that constitutes a human being continues to exist after death. However, they would not wish to be specific about how, where, or in what form. They might talk in terms of the soul or spirit returning to God. They might say that the essence of a person is rewoven into the spiritual life of the universe, just as the body's constituents are reworked into the universe's physical dimension. Some are interested in exploring the various theories of reincarnation. The persistence of a person's ideas, genes, and more intangible influences would be as much as many Unitarians would be prepared to concede. Some prefer to say nothing at all, being content to "take one world at a time". Most, though, would also point to the continued existence of individuals in the memories and lives of those who knew and loved them, and would see in this a source of comfort.

Whatever our position, most Unitarians agree that this is an area of mystery. Many theories exist, many claims are made, but undisputed evidence is hard to find. Unitarians take the view that, in any case, the focus of our attention should be this world. Our concern is better directed to considering how we should live our lives in the here and now. A life well-lived is the best preparation for death, whatever may lie beyond it.

Cliff Reed [269]

In the struggles we choose for ourselves, in the ways we move forward in our lives and bring our way forward with us, it is right to remember the names of those who gave us strength in this choice of living. It is right to name the power of hard lives well lived. We share a history with those lives. We belong to the same motion. They too were strengthened by what had gone before. They too were drawn on by the vision of what might come to be.

Those who lived before us, who struggled for justice and suffered injustice before us, have not melted into the dust, and have not disappeared. They are with us still. The lives they lived hold us steady. Their words remind us and call us back to ourselves. Their courage and love evoke our own. We, the living, carry them with us: we are their voices, their hands and their hearts. We take them with us, and with them choose the deeper path of living.

Kathleen McTigue [270]

The lessons of living and dying are intertwined. We believe that the pursuit of wisdom, as Socrates puts it, essentially entails the practice of dying: learning how to let go of issues and possessions, shedding illusions, pruning regrets, dropping grudges, saying farewell to our dearest notions and closest ties. We practice some dying every day, so that when we reach our physical end, we will be in reasonably good spiritual shape and with Pope John be able to declare: "My bags are packed, and I am ready to go!"

Tom Owen-Towle [271]

The ideal way of achieving an appropriate funeral is for each individual to draft an outline, in advance, of their own funeral service. A number of Unitarians (including myself) have done this, and the practice is encouraging and growing. Care is needed to ensure that those who take part in such a service are allowed their own distinctive contribution, but appropriate foresight ensures that one receives an appropriate farewell. In my own case, I would particularly wish to avoid a funeral where – as commonly happens

– the tribute elevated me to the status of a saint: while it might be equally inappropriate to enumerate my many shortcomings, I would at least hope for a realistic appraisal on death! Other Unitarians, no doubt, have their own particular desires, which can be met when due forethought is given.

George Chryssides [272]

[Elhanan Winchester's] death was fast approaching, and he contemplated it with serenity and joy. On the morning of his decease, he requested two or three young ladies, who were sitting by him, to join in singing a hymn, observing at the same time that he might expire before it should be finished. He began with them; but his voice soon faltered, and the torpor of death fell upon him. They were disconcerted, and paused; but he, reviving, encouraged them to proceed, and joined in the first line of each stanza until he breathed no more.

Thomas Whittemore [273]

I used to be always thinking about death – partly from taste, and partly as a duty. And now that I am waiting it at any hour, the whole thing seems so easy, simple and natural that I cannot but wonder how I could keep my thoughts fixed upon it when it was far off. I cannot do it now... I find death in prospect the simplest thing in the world – a thing not to be feared or regretted, or to get excited about in any way... Sympathy with those who will miss me, I do feel of course: yet not very painfully, because their sorrow cannot, in the nature of things, long interfere with their daily peace; but to me there is no sacrifice, no sense of loss, nothing to fear, nothing to regret. Under the eternal laws of the universe I came into being, and, under them, I have lived a life so full that its fullness is equivalent to length.

Harriet Martineau [274]

Friendship

Sometimes our light goes out but is blown into flame by an encounter with another human being. Each of us owes the deepest thanks to those who have rekindled this inner light.

Albert Schweitzer [275]

The only way to have a friend is to be one.

Ralph Waldo Emerson [276]

Several lesbian theologians have developed theologies of friendship. Often queer people do not find acceptance in their original families, so they have to make friendships and support networks in order to survive... justice-making friendship... This friendship is available to everyone... The Church is seen as a coalition of justice-seeking friends.

Ann Peart [277]

Chronic loneliness and lack of love can kill you faster than anything else in the world. Relationships, the state of them, the nurturance of them, the maintenance of them, the willingness to be vulnerable and to be tender, they tell you a lot about your well-being and your ability to heal.

Stephen Kendrick [278]

Sex and sexuality

Unitarians see human sexuality as a perfectly natural and healthy dimension of our existence.

Although it is fundamentally the means of pro-creation, Unitarians recognise and value its role in bringing intimacy, tenderness, and pleasure to loving relationships. We do not insist that sex is for procreative purposes only, but its primeval purpose is a source of wonder, reverence, and awe.

For the most part, Unitarians take the view that the natural spectrum of sexuality includes both homosexuality and bisexuality. For this reason we would affirm the right of gay, lesbian, and bisexual people to give full emotional and physical expression to their sexuality.

In all matters relating to sexuality, however, Unitarians stress the absolute necessity of responsibility and respect. For us, sexual immorality means any form of sexual activity that is not conducted on a sure basis of mutual consent and with due regard to the health, welfare, and feelings of third parties. Unitarians regard sexual abuse and exploitation of any kind as an affront to the rights, worth, and dignity of the human person. Any sexual activity that is not entered into willingly, consciously, respectfully, and lovingly by consenting and responsible adults is seen by Unitarians as dangerous and unacceptable.

In our view sex, properly used, is a wonderful gift to be thankful for. If, however, it is squandered or used to degrade and hurt others, then something wonderful becomes tawdry and squalid.

Cliff Reed [279]

Love is supposed to be the very essence of religion – love of God, love of truth, love of wisdom and justice, love of one's neighbour as oneself. Desire and passion, however, have been much more problematic. A religion that prides itself on being rational gives but limited expression to such feelings. It is only in worship material, mainly hymns, that emotions are allowed to show...

Unitarians have written much about reason, rights, and responsibilities, but little about passion and emotion, even less about sexuality... Sexuality... is a universal given of the human condition. How it is experienced, described, and valued varies enormously among cultures, both in the present and throughout human history.

Ann Peart [280]

Belonging to the order of creation, sexuality – in the biblical view – is of course in essence good... Without it, life could not continue, and in its proper use it brings about a union between man and woman which provides a gracious and unique fulfillment. On the other hand, it is subject to an infinite variety of distortions and frustrations...

The intercourse that makes two people into one body is imbued with the love of one for the other. It is without its proper meaning unless it consummates love in its various dimensions, and unless it expresses the recognition of the ontological change in the man and the woman and in their relation to each other, a change that gives rise to a special vocation of togetherness under God...

James Luther Adams [281]

Marriage

The marriage bond, like all personal relations, is a relationship between individuals... Human persons are not like peas in a pod. Each has her or his own individuality. Yet, each individual is also a person. These facts become especially evident in marriage; they give to marriage many of its peculiar opportunities and responsibilities, and many of its special problems...

Marriage... is a bond within the context of the larger covenant, of a covenant of the community of faith under God...

The covenant of marriage is not merely a family covenant. It is a circle within, and integrally related to, the concentric circles of the larger communities of participation and responsibility. If it were not, it would be the enemy of justice and peace, a restrictive covenant.

Ultimately of course the covenant of marriage, like the covenant of the community of faith, is not rooted in a sense of responsibility under a stern god of duty. It is rooted in a love that is stronger than passion, stronger than the slings and arrows of fortune...

The covenant of marriage is rooted in the affection, the magic bond, that holds the world together. It is rooted in the covenant of being itself.

James Luther Adams [282]

I am often called upon to officiate at rites of passage for less than conventional situations, e.g. same-sex blessings, different-sex blessings (as opposed to legal marriages), the adoption of a child, the birth of a child to same-sex couples and to single mothers, marriages of couples representing different faith or racial backgrounds. These services are clear manifestations of the Unitarian respect for diversity.

Jeffrey Gould [283]

As same-sex partnerships are not recognised as marriages (with all their underpinnings of patriarchy and sexism), gay men and lesbians are free to invent their own relationships. Although some same-sex couples do refer to their relationship as marriage, many seek other models of developing an ethical partnership. Same-sex couples have the advantage of not having to cope with gender inequalities, so there is a greater possibility of mutuality and genuine equality.

Ann Peart [284]

The Internet introduces a new set of relationships between individuals... we may communicate with scores of people from all over the world... How should we view a married person who establishes a relationship with someone of the opposite sex over the Internet? ... Is it infidelity to one's partner? Or is it up to each couple to decide for themselves what is and is not permissible?

Tony Cann and George Chryssides [285]

It takes years to marry completely two hearts, even of the most loving and well assorted. A happy wedlock is a long falling in love. Young persons think love belongs only to the brown-haired and crimson-cheeked. So it does for its beginning. But the golden marriage is a part of love which the bridal day knows nothing of ...

Such a large and sweet fruit is a complete marriage that it needs a long summer to ripen in, and then a long winter to mellow and season in. But a real, happy marriage of love and judgment between a noble man and woman is one of the things so very handsome that if the sun were, as the Greek poets fabled, a god, he might stop the world and hold it still now and then, in order to look all day long on some example thereof, and feast his eyes on such a spectacle.

Theodore Parker [286]

I hope we can ask ourselves why marriage matters... and whether we want to help UU married couples achieve the audacious goal of a loving, lifelong union in the bosom of a community of faith and practice...

Now after thirty-three years of marriage to the same woman and a career working with couples in distress, I see lifelong marriage as a countercultural act in a throwaway society. Without ignoring the shadow side of marriage and the pain of divorces that cannot be avoided, we religious liberals can support marriage and shape its future according to liberal ideals...

I now see divorce as a sometimes-necessary evil to prevent greater evil in a toxic marriage or to end an already-dead marriage, but not as a sacrament of personal liberation....

We Unitarian Universalists will always be liberationists – it's in our heritage and our haemoglobin. But today's freedom struggle for marriage is not against the chains of marriage that bind people in a stifling grasp, but against the Velcro marriage that gives way too quickly in the face of the inevitable pulling and wrenching of mates working out a life together. The struggle now is against what I call consumer marriage, the invasion of market values into the intimate sphere of life...

More than anything else, I believe we need a Unitarian Universalist view of marriage that combines our traditional strengths in individual freedom, our more recently acquired affirmations of gender equality and equality by sexual orientation, and the new ground we will have to plow to develop a theology of commitment, spiritual growth, and public and private covenant in marriage.

William J. Doherty [287]

Family

Recognizing our ministry to families and communities as a core mission of UU congregations, we need to develop philosophy, resources, programs, and networks to serve and service this mission. Often our ministry is focused on the individual (commitment to the inherent worth and dignity of every person), overshadowing our ministry to families and to the whole congregational community (commitment to justice, equity, compassion, and responsibility). Worship, education, social action, and fellowship are components of ministry wherein the whole community is nurtured through ongoing conversations between leaders and congregants of all ages. Our ministry needs to celebrate all kinds of families, educate on family issues and UU values, advocate for family social justice, and companion our families with links between church and home.

Unitarian Universalist General Assembly 2005 Theme: Ministering to Families in Today's World [288]

The family cannot escape providing religious instruction for its children. Religious education goes on all the time – in the way the family treats outsiders, neighbors, help, workmen, in the family attitudes toward foreigners and strangers, and in their attitudes towards one another. Religious education is implicit in the method used in solving problems in the family and in the way decisions are made. The quality of religious instruction is evident in the response of family members to small creatures – to snakes, bees, frogs, beetles; it is apparent in the way they treat dogs and cats, whether their own or someone else's, or just strays. They provide still another facet of religious instruction in their attitude toward music and art and in the type of response they make to the television programs that express violence, disregard of human values, unfair representations of husband–wife relationships, and lack of moral sensitivity and intellectual awareness.

A family can further its own religious growth by taking an honest look at the kind of responses each member makes to the ordinary situations of daily life – during the early morning rush to get off to school and work, for instance, or at the dinner table – and at the differences in response when members are under stress or in the midst of an emergency. Furthermore, the family can look for opportunities in everyday life to foster religious growth and strengthen its constructive attitudes.

As part of the everyday routine, are there opportunities for children to throw off tensions and relax? Have parents time to listen to children's enthusiasms and their troubles? Is there a period for the whole family to be together so that parents and children can enjoy each other's company? Are there chances to be together on all levels, from chores to fun? Is there a pattern of freedom and democracy, of responsibility and discipline, so that they do not deny one another, but establish an orderly, consistent pattern for the development of values?

George N. Marshall [289]

Responsibilities

It is often supposed that guilt is a thing essentially exclusive –
attaching only to those who are immediately responsible for wrong.
But it is a necessary aspect of our life as members of society that we
share a common responsibility and therefore a common guilt.

A Free Religious Faith: The Report of the Unitarian Commission [290]

Despair is my private pain
Born from what I have failed to say
failed to do, failed to overcome.
Be still my inner self
let me rise to you, let me reach down into your pain
and soothe you.
I turn to you to renew my life
I turn to the world, the streets of the city, the worn tapestries of
    brokerage firms,
drug dealers, private estates
personal things in the bag lady's cart
rage and pain in the faces that turn from me
afraid of their own inner worlds.
This common world I love anew,
as the life blood of generations
who refuse to surrender their humanity
in an inhumane world
courses through my veins.
From within this world
my despair is transformed to hope
and I begin anew
the legacy of caring.

Thandeka [291]

The Free Christian's sense of responsibility in society issues from concern for something more than the desire for personal success. It issues from the experience of and the demand for community. For the Free Christian, responsibility is a response to the Deed that was "in the beginning", to the deed of *Agape* that originally gave birth to the Christian community. It is a response to that divine, self-giving, sacrificial love which creates and continually transforms a community of persons. This response by which community is formed and transformed is a process whereby men and women in obedience, freedom and fellowship come to know God and to enjoy him. Responsibility is response to a divinely given community-forming power; the early Christians spoke of it as "living in Christ", as God's pouring forth of His spirit...

Thus every personal problem is a social problem, and every social problem is a personal problem.

James Luther Adams [292]

Evil is related to emptiness. It fills a void. Where good is not consciously active and diligent, evil enters... Let us accept our responsibility with more grace than guilt. Thinking collectively, let our liberal religious community remember that we are a part of the whole, and if the whole is wounded we are wounded as well.

Elizabeth Ellis-Hagler [293]

Giving, economics, and poverty

We say that revelation is not sealed, but we often act as if our purses were... How many of our ministers serve congregations where the live income funds a proper stipend for the minister? Simplifying somewhat, a congregation of 100 requires an average annual contribution of 1% gross income from each member to provide the minister with an income equal to the average of the congregation; a congregation of 40 needs an average contribution of 2.5%, and a congregation of 20 needs 5%. And this is just for the minister's stipend, not the cost of the whole ministry of the church.

If we see ministry as hiring someone to do ministry for us because we have some spiritual duty towards the world, this will be very different from seeing the called minister (or lay pastor or lay leader) as joining our religious community to help us to do our ministering. One reflection of this difference will be in our valuing of our support of our ministry...

The value that each of you places on your local congregation and the situational stretching or squeezing that affects the actual amount you contribute is for each individual to judge, but I firmly believe that our congregations will never thrive until we support our own ministry. In words mostly of one syllable, one reason why we are such poor givers is that too many of us see the ministry of our church as the job of someone we call a minister rather than as OUR, personal, ministry.

John Clifford [294]

Give what you have. To someone it may be better than you dare to think.

Henry Wadsworth Longfellow [295]

Men are judged by what is given, not what is withheld.

Theodore Parker [296]

One may give without loving, but none can love without giving.

Anonymous [297]

Conflicts over access to natural resources, such as oil or water, are likely to become a commoner cause of war, as population growth and living standards put pressure on natural resources. The free-market economic system – the dominant ideology of our world as we enter the twenty-first century – produces, as a natural product of its operation, inequality of income and wealth, and this is another potential source of conflict, both within States and between them. State-directed economies are seen as failures, but the free-market system is deeply flawed also. It requires to be brought under greater democratic control than is currently the case. Perhaps even profounder, however, is the need to change from efforts to promote an ever-expanding economy to the creation of one that is sustainable in the long term, taking account of limited natural resources and the polluting side-effects of intensive economic processes.

George Paxton [298]

A number of years ago I woke up to the fact that much of the money that drives the stock exchanges of the world came from the pension schemes of people like you and me. No longer could I merely blame rich capitalists! I had to discover what responsibility I was prepared to take for the ways my pension money was being put to work in the world, and to accept the fact that I probably have more power to change the world through my pension contributions than through my election vote. But how hard I find it to continue taking active responsibility for something that feels so distant and the connections so impersonal.

Peter Hawkins [299]

My next remark concerns not only the rich capitalist, but people of moderate means, who are willing to give, and every year do give something, for the relief of poverty and the eradication of vice. To these I would say, so disburse your money that it will not feed idleness, but excite the poor to maintain themselves. I have said that those who dwell in the Lower Depths require not charity, but justice.

Edwin H. Chapin [300]

Suffering occurs not because the Cosmos wills it, seeks it, or chooses pain; poverty, in all its forms (e.g. economic, spiritual, or emotional), is part of Life's repertoire of responses initiated by humankind's neglect – from our abuse of each other and the Cosmos...

To speak of *God's* preferential option for the poor is to work for balance while recognizing limits, which is the nature of the Cosmos (which is God)... Acting on behalf of the oppressed, the poor, is working for balance within limits...

As members of the North Atlantic community, Unitarian Universalists (and others) are in a unique position. Largely white, well educated, and financially secure (this is to say, socially comfortable), Unitarian Universalists must act on the preferential option for life. We must take the lead by choosing life, by being "good neighbors", an option not available to everyone...

Our responsibility is clear. It means choosing a preferential option for the poor by choosing balance and limits, the essence of the Cosmos; it means siding with life so that all people can live unoppressed and live with the benefits of humanization.

Fredric John Muir [301]

Commitment, action, and service

I am only one, but still I am one. I cannot do everything, but still I can do something. And because I cannot do everything I will not refuse to do the something that I can do.

Edward Everett Hale [302]

What good is it, my brothers and sisters, if you say you have faith, but do not have works? Can faith save you? If a brother or sister is naked and lacks daily food, and one of you says to them, "Go in peace; keep warm and eat your fill", and yet you do not supply their bodily needs, what is the good of that? So faith by itself, if it has no works, is dead.

The Letter of James [303]

Commit yourself equally to your worshipping community, to your District, and to the Assembly – for resurgence in the movement can only come through conviction and faith at grass roots.

Anonymous [304]

The element of commitment, of change of heart, of decision, so much emphasized in the Gospels, has been neglected by religious liberalism, and that is the prime source of its enfeeblement. We liberals are largely an uncommitted and therefore a self-frustrating people. Our first task, then, is to restore to liberalism its own dynamic and its own prophetic genius. We need conversion within ourselves.

James Luther Adams [305]

To know what is right, and to pursue it independently of public opinion or of censure, is a high characteristic, and one that we should individually strive to attain.

Emily Howard Jennings Stowe [306]

There is no limit to what can be accomplished if it doesn't matter who gets the credit.

Ralph Waldo Emerson [307]

Be not simply good; be good for something.

Henry David Thoreau [308]

Universalists are concerned about tomorrow and work ceaselessly to make society more beautiful and just, but we relinquish the final results. There is a rabbinical tale to the effect that theology means brooding over what God is worrying about when God arises in the morning. Well, if anything, God stews about repairing creation's brokenness. If that's true, then that's precisely what we humans ought to be worrying about too, concerned enough to do our share of the mending. But we should not be so worried that we cannot let go of our outcomes and efforts, surrendering them back to the mystery from whence we came. For what ultimately holds us, no matter what we have accomplished or failed to accomplish on earth, is a loving God.

Tom Owen-Towle [309]

If we suffer in the pursuit of our life-work, of that which we consider good and right; if we suffer for the sake of principle and are prepared to risk everything for that principle, loss of outward goods, of position, influence, taking upon ourselves slander, shame, ignominy, death if need be; then our suffering beareth fruit unto life...not for ourselves only, but for others also, for the generation that now is, and maybe for untold generations to come.

Gertrude von Petzold [310]

Do we believe that simply to think about an issue is the same as to live in a way which exemplifies our concern for the issue?

Thandeka [311]

Justice and confronting evil

The vision of the Kingdom of God, a global commonwealth of peace, justice and plenty for all, has always been important for Unitarians. It has inspired their social and political involvement, duly tempered by a realistic assessment of what can be achieved.

"Standing for Common Values", General Assembly of Unitarian and Free Christian Churches [312]

We... declare the primal task of the church of to-day to be the reconstruction of the world's civilization in terms of justice, peace and righteousness, so that the spiritual life of all may develop to its fullest capacity.

"A Social Program", Report of the National Commission of the Universalist Church [313]

What does the LORD require of you but to do justice, and to love kindness, and to walk humbly with your God?

The Prophet Micah [314]

Resistance to tyranny is obedience to God.

Susan B. Anthony [315]

Kindness without justice is of little moral worth.

William Ellery Channing [316]

The long-term causes of war and the deeper underlying causes could be described as the lack of justice and equality in society, and inherited mental attitudes and ideologies. Anything we do to make our world society a more just and tolerant community – and therefore a more coherent society – will help to reduce the likelihood of conflicts which may develop into violence.

George Paxton [317]

The mandatory first step in addressing evil is to acknowledge our own complicity in it. Before fighting it in the outside world, we must recognize palpable evil in our picayune malices and stealthy deceits, our unworthy fears and hurtful hostilities, displayed both privately and publicly.

Tom Owen-Towle [318]

The arc of the universe is long, but it bends toward justice.

Theodore Parker [319]

One of the most obvious things in contemplating these Lower Depths of Vice and Poverty is the fact that mere *Education* is not a sufficient remedy. Religious teaching is not enough. Do not think, for a single moment, that I under-estimate it. I know that the moral power which religion imparts is mighty over external circumstances, and that there is not true reformation unless its regenerating life strikes into the very centre of the heart... [But] We do say, that tracts, and Bibles, and religious conversation will be but little heeded by those who are too numb with cold, and perishing with hunger; that in order to get at their inner nature, a thick crust of physical misery must be removed... So these, in the Lower Depths of the great City, who *are* fainting by the way, must be restored with bread and meat; these who are shivering with the winter's frost must be warmed and clothed; and we must reach their deepest nature – intellectual and moral – by removing that cramp of physical position, that craving of physical need, which they most distinctly feel.

Edwin H. Chapin [320]

There must be more equality established in society, or morality will never gain ground, and this virtuous equality will not rest firmly even when founded on a rock, if one-half of mankind be chained to its bottom by fate.

Mary Wollstonecraft [321]

Reconciliation and forgiveness

Determined to destroy the Buddha, a treacherous demon unleashed an elephant, which charged drunkenly at the Buddha. Just as the furious beast was about to trample him, the Buddha raised his right hand with fingers held close together and open palm facing the oncoming animal. This fearless gesture stopped the elephant in its tracks and completely subdued the dangerous creature.

Once having faced the terrible threat of annihilation, the compassionate Buddha extended his other hand with its palm up, as if cupping the gift of an open heart. This charitable gesture of forgiveness restored the elephant's natural tranquillity. And so proceeds our human passage: hands thrust in resistance *and* hands offered in conciliation.

Tom Owen-Towle [322]

As Unitarian Christians who believe in the one all-encompassing God and our oneness with him, I suggest it is our duty to act on this belief... and counterbalance this growing polarisation of society. Jesus Christ said, "Blessed are the peacemakers, for they shall be called sons of God" (Matthew 5:9). Paul followed this in Corinthians 7:15, speaking of how God "reconciled us to Himself through Christ, and gave us the ministry of reconciliation". It is my belief that the Unitarian response to the growing clash between civilizations should be that of "reconciler" and "peacemaker".

First we must make peace with ourselves and reconcile our own beliefs with that of Jesus. In these times even the best of us will be prone to prejudices and anger at what we see on our TV screens, on websites and in the newspapers. We should follow the teachings of Jesus when he says, "Love your enemies" (Matthew 5:44; Luke 6:27), "Do not resist him that is wicked; but whoever slaps you on your right cheek, turn to him the other also" (Matthew 5:39) and, alternately, "To him that strikes you on the cheek, offer the other also" (Luke 6:29). This message is not one of submission but one of dignified strength; instead of responding in kind to hatred, prejudice and violence, we must engage in an inner struggle to tackle our own prejudices, stand firm with our Christian principles and be willing to experience more hatred and violence for doing so. We must be prepared to weather the storm and not get swept along with the madness that humanity engages in.

Matt Grant [323]

The remedy for sin is a process of contrition, repentance, and forgiveness. That is, true regret, a turning away from what conscience condemns, and a loving acceptance of the sinner. The giving and receiving of forgiveness – including self-forgiveness – are necessary for healing to take place. Through forgiveness (human or divine) the wholeness and fellowship that sin fractures are restored. Unitarians believe that we must always be ready to forgive. It is no part of our practice to load people with guilt. A burden of guilt is destructive both spiritually and psychologically.

Cliff Reed [324]

Practicing reconciliation is my personal spiritual discipline. As a management consultant, I know a lot about helping people work through their differences, but until I embraced reconciliation as a spiritual practice, I didn't realize just how transformative reconciliation can be. Practicing reconciliation means I commit to being in right relationship with people in my life and, when I'm not, caring enough to face unresolved issues and improve the relationship. I keep two lists: One has the names of people with whom I need to reconcile. The other has names of people with whom I have begun reconciliation efforts. The lists keep my commitment in front of me. Each time I am able to move forward with another person, I draw a line through her or his name on the list of people with whom reconciliation is needed—and the list of people with whom I have begun reconciliation grows longer...

I have learned to practice reconciliation in my personal relationships... I have also been learning to practice reconciliation across divides in our broken culture, especially racial divides. I have carried reconciliation with me while working in All Souls Church in Washington, where I am a lifelong member, and increasingly in the Unitarian Universalist Association at large. From this experience I have learned that reconciliation is a competency we can bring to four levels of conflict—in our own souls, between individuals... within groups like my congregation, and between groups such as people of color like me and the dominant white culture. Reconciliation helps us to get into right relationship.

Paula Cole Jones [325]

Change and the future

At no time can you say, "The world is this", for before you have finished saying it, the world has changed.

Michael Servetus [326]

Not everything that is old is good, just as not everything that is new is false.

George Enyedi [327]

I have an almost complete disregard of precedent and a faith in the possibility of something better. It irritates me to be told how things have always been done . . . I defy the tyranny of precedent. I cannot afford the luxury of a closed mind. I go for anything new that might improve the past.

Clara Barton [328]

Far from having nothing to say, religious liberals have to proclaim, over and over again, against both religious and secular adversaries, the good news that the future remains open and the Fates are not in control.

Gene Reeves [329]

The wisdom of one generation will ever be the folly of the next.

Joseph Priestley [330]

To build high – dig deep.

Cross Street Chapel, Manchester [331]

We need spiritual giants in the earth who dare to break the shackles of the past; creative, onward-looking pioneers, who dare to go forward.

Clarence Skinner [332]

I believe that we are here to some purpose, that the purpose has something to do with the future, and that it transcends altogether the limits of our present knowledge and understanding. If you like, you can call the transcendent purpose God. If it is God, it is a Socinian God, inherent in the universe and growing in power and knowledge as the universe unfolds. Our minds are not only expressions of its purpose but are also contributions to its growth.

Freeman Dyson [333]

There is nothing rigid or static in ... nature, humanity or society. Everything is in motion, fluctuating and changing. So-called stillness is only a transient state in the movement towards new forms of being. To be and to move have the same meaning. Hearts pulsate continuously and when they stop, even then they do not rest. There is enormous movement as the particles of the body crumble into dust. The law of eternal, never-ceasing change is valid not only for the material but also for the spiritual life – and the latter to an even greater extent. If there is no lack of movement in material existence, how much less can there be in spiritual life? If the everlasting, flowing processes of nature cannot be stopped, how much less possible is it to do so with spiritual energies? If one engages in such a task, one proposes the impossible for oneself. And yet there were and are such people.

People do exist who obstruct the course of the universal and rhythmical progress of spiritual life by building barriers across its immense course, trying to obstruct its swell, attempting to arrest its eternal movement, trying to coerce into stillness eternally changing human thought. From that imprudent nascence dogmatism was, and is, born.

Imre Gellérd [334]

We are, many of us, in these days wandering far and wide in despairing search for some bread of life whereby we may sustain our souls, some *Holy Grail* wherein we may drink salvation from doubt and sin. It may be a long, long quest ere we find it; but one thing is ready to our hands. It is *duty*. Let us turn to that in simple fidelity, and labour to act up to our own highest ideals, to *be* the very best and purest and truest we know how, and to *do* around us every work of love which our hands and hearts may reach. When we have lived and laboured like this, then, I believe, that the light will come to us, as to many another doubting soul; and it will prove true once more that "they who do God's will shall know of his doctrine", and they who strive to advance his kingdom here will gain faith in another divine realm beyond the dark river, where Virtue shall ascend into Holiness, and Duty be transfigured into Joy.

Frances Power Cobbe [335]

There are times when I stand aside and wonder at the strangeness of this world of ours. The years of all of us are short, our lives precarious. Our days and nights go hurrying on and there is scarcely time to do the little that we might. Yet we find time for bitterness, for petty treason and evasion. What can we do to stretch our hearts enough to lose their littleness? Here we are – all of us – all of us upon this planet, bound together in a common destiny, living our lives between the briefness of the daylight and the dark. Kindred in this, each lighted by the same precarious, flickering flame of life, how does it happen that we are not kindred in all things else? How strange and foolish are these walls of separation that divide us! ... When I think of these things, I wonder. I wonder at the patience of God. While the dream still lives in our hearts, God waits. While the vision shines in our eyes, God hopes. How long shall we keep God waiting?

A. Powell Davies [336]

The Unitarian philosophy is uniquely equipped to provide a coherent, caring, religious approach in the twenty-first century. But if we do not leap out of the rut we have got into, we will stay stuck in it, and the movement will decline and die. We have the ideas, the freedom, and the resources to secure the future, if we can only decide to take our courage in both hands and go for it.

Anonymous [337]

Biographical notes

Aaronson, Jane (p. 74) is a member of St. Mark's Unitarian Church, Edinburgh.

Acuay, Hafidha (p. 23) lives in Portland, Oregon. She is active in Unitarian Universalist young adult activities in North America.

Adams, James Luther (1901–1994) (pp. 22, 41, 42, 90, 119, 129, 147, 156, 157, 163, 167) was perhaps the most prominent thinker in twentieth-century Unitarianism. A minister, theologian, and social ethicist, he studied in Germany in the 1930s and worked with the underground church, resisting Nazism.

Adams, Sarah Flower (1805–1848) (p. 142) was a hymn writer and poet. She attended the South Place Unitarian Church, Finsbury, London.

Anthony, Susan B. (1820–1906) (pp. 19, 169) was an ardent activist for temperance, the abolition of slavery, and women's rights. Originally a Quaker, she later became a Unitarian.

Argow, Waldemar (1891–1961) (p. 22) was an American author, poet, and Unitarian minister.

Backus, E. Burdette (1888–1955) (p. 17) was an American Unitarian minister, humanist, and civil-rights activist.

Ballou, Hosea (1771–1852) (p. 36) was the most influential Universalist preacher of his time. He was reared as a Baptist and became a Universalist at the age of 19. He was a minister in New England, where his religious views attracted controversy.

Barbauld, Anna Laetitia Aikin (1743–1825) (pp. 45, 143) was a Unitarian poet, hymn writer, and abolitionist.

Barton, Clara (1821–1912) (p. 174) was a Universalist, teacher, nurse, and founder of the American Red Cross.

Bate, Allistair (p. 87) is a former Lay Leader in Charge of the Glasgow Unitarian congregation.

Belletini, Mark (p. 42) is Senior Minister of the First Unitarian Universalist Church of Columbus, Ohio, USA.

de Benneville, George (1703–1793) (pp. 31, 57, 142) was a Universalist mystic and preacher who preached throughout Europe and the New World.

Biddle, John (1615–1662) (pp. 90, 95) is considered the "father of English Unitarianism", although he did not live to see an organised Unitarian movement. For his anti-Trinitarian preaching he was arrested and imprisoned many times. He died from an illness contracted while in prison.

Blackwell, Elizabeth (1821–1910) (pp. 33, 150) was born in England and later moved to the United States, where she became America's first female doctor in 1849. She promoted health and hygiene in England and the United States throughout her life.

Bodichon, Barbara Leigh Smith (1827–1891) (p. 93) was active in the women's suffrage movement and founded the progressive Portman Hall School.

Boeke, Johanna (p. 91) is a Unitarian minister who has served churches in southern England and California.

Bowens-Wheatley, Marjorie (1949–2006) (p. 29) was a founding member of the African American Unitarian Universalist Ministry.

Bray McNatt, Rosemary (p. 68) is minister of The Fourth Universalist Society in the City of New York.

von Britzke, Michaela (pp. 45, 76, 131) is a German-born psychotherapist living in London. She is a member of Essex Unitarian Church, Kensington, London.

Brown, Andrew (pp. 97, 120) is minister of Cambridge Unitarian Church.

Brown, Leni (p. 70) is a member of First Unitarian Society Plainfield, New Jersey.

Brown, Olympia (1835–1926) (pp. 15, 47, 108) was ordained as a Universalist minister in 1863: the first woman ordained to the ministry with full denominational authority in America. She was active in the women's suffrage movement.

Buehrens, John (pp. 39, 99) was the sixth president of the Unitarian Universalist Association from 1993 to 2001. He is the author, with Forrest Church, of *A Chosen Faith: An Introduction to Unitarian Universalism.*

Call, Lon Ray (1894–1985) (p. 138) was a Unitarian minister, instrumental in the Fellowship movement, which contributed to a significant growth in American Unitarianism.

Cann, Tony (pp. 102, 158) is a Director of the University for Industry. He is involved in computing and education and has been a Unitarian since he was a student.

Capek, Norbert F. (1870–1942) (p. 54) founded the Czech Unitarian Church after he became a Unitarian while in the United States. He created the "Flower Communion", which is used widely in Unitarian churches. He was martyred at Dachau concentration camp in 1942.

Carnes, Paul (1921–1979) (pp. 36, 76) was the third president of the Unitarian Universalist Association.

Carpenter, Joseph Estlin (1844–1927) (p. 135) was a Unitarian minister and scholar, and the first president of the International Association for Religious Freedom, the oldest international interfaith organisation in the world.

Carrier, Gaston M. (p. 138) is a Unitarian Universalist minister.

Channing, William Ellery (1780–1842) (pp. 21, 76, 88, 113, 118, 169) is considered "the father of American Unitarianism". A Boston minister, his sermon in 1819 entitled "Unitarian Christianity" is considered one of the most important sermons in Unitarian history.

Chapin, Edwin H. (1814–1880) (pp. 166, 170) was a Universalist minister.

Chryssides, George (pp. 49, 51, 56, 57, 102, 153, 158) is Head of Religious Studies at the University of Wolverhampton and author of *Exploring New Religions* and *The Elements of Unitarianism*.

Clifford, John (pp. 26, 28, 32, 51, 58, 164) is the Executive Secretary of the International Council of Unitarians and Universalists and was for 12 years the Deputy General Secretary of the General Assembly of Unitarian and Free Christian Churches.

Cobbe, Frances Power (1822–1904) (pp. 104, 176) was one of the most influential figures in British Unitarianism in the nineteenth century. She worked tirelessly for the emancipation of women, social and educational reform, and animal welfare.

Cockroft, Lena (p. 92) is a minister and former Moderator of the Non-Subscribing Presbyterian Church of Ireland.

Cowan, Roger (1929–2002) (p. 22) was a Unitarian Universalist minister. He was active in politics and civil liberties.

Crawford, Alma Faith (p. 34) is Associate Professor of Preaching and Worship at Starr King School for the Ministry in California. In 1996 she co-founded Church of the Open Door, a Unitarian Universalist urban ministry serving more than 200 African American and immigrant families.

Crawford Harvie, Kim K. (p. 69) is Senior Minister of Arlington Street Church in Boston.

Croft, Joy (p. 123) is a Unitarian minister and former president of the Unitarian Peace Fellowship.

Cummins, Drusilla (p. 142) is a former president of the Unitarian Universalist Women's Federation.

Curren, Vina (p. 79) is a Unitarian lay pastor living in Bolton.

Darlison, Bill (pp. 34, 46, 117) is minister of Dublin Unitarian Church.

David, Francis (Ferencz) (1510–1579) (pp. 12, 118, 131) is considered the founder of Unitarianism in Transylvania. He converted the ruler of Transylvania, Prince Sigismund, to Unitarianism, but after Sigismund's death David and Unitarianism fell out of favour with the authorities and David was arrested and later died in prison.

Davies, A. Powell (1902–1957) (pp. 18, 31, 77, 78, 92, 130, 131, 140, 176) was born in England but emigrated to the United States in 1928. Originally a Methodist minister, he converted to Unitarianism in 1932. As a minister in Washington, DC, he worked against racial segregation and planted many Unitarian churches, as well as preaching against Senator McCarthy's persecution of Communist Party members.

Dennison, Sean (p. 69) is the minister of South Valley Unitarian Universalist Society in Salt Lake City, Utah.

Dobbs, Lynn (p. 71) is a social-justice activist and a member of First Unitarian Universalist Church of San Diego, California.

Doherty, William J. (p. 159) is the director of the marriage and family therapy programme at the University of Minnesota. He is a member of the First Universalist Church of Minneapolis.

Dyson, Freeman (p. 175) is an English-born American physicist and mathematician. In 2000 he received the Templeton Prize for progress in religion.

Ellis-Hagler, Elizabeth (p. 163) is a Unitarian Universalist minister, formerly with the Unitarian Universalist Urban Ministry in Boston.

Emerson, Ralph Waldo (1803–1882) (pp. 90, 96, 100, 119, 130, 134, 137, 154, 168) was a Unitarian minister, essayist, and philosopher. An important American literary figure, he was an instigator of the Transcendentalist movement, opening Unitarianism to science, Eastern religions, and naturalistic mysticism.

Engel, J. Ronald (p. 105) is a Unitarian Universalist minister and a former professor of social ethics at Meadville Lombard Theological School in Chicago.

Enyedi, George (Gyorgy) (pp. 54, 174) was a scholar, minister, and superintendent of the Transylvanian Unitarian Church. He died in 1597.

Fahs, Sophia Lyon (1876–1978) (p. 127) was a religious educator who edited innovative curriculum material for the American Unitarian Association.

Fewkes, Richard is a Unitarian Universalist minister.

Ford, James Ishmael (p. 62) is senior minister of the First Unitarian Society in Newton, Massachusetts and a Buddhist Zen master. He is the founder of the Boundless Way Zen Community, and the lead teacher for the Henry Thoreau Zen Sangha.

Fuller, Margaret (1810–1850) (p. 28) was a feminist writer and Transcendentalist.

Gellérd, Imre (1920–1980) (pp. 22, 89, 132, 175) was a Transylvanian Unitarian minister who suffered imprisonment under the Communist regime for his writings.

Gould, Jeffrey (pp. 70, 157) is the minister of the Bury and Ainsworth Unitarian congregations.

Grant, Matt (pp. 57, 172) is a member of the Unitarian Christian Association, with interests in Panentheism and Zen Buddhism.

Griffith, Rosemary (p. 86) is a Unitarian lay preacher and theologian.

Hale, Edward Everett (1822–1909) (p. 167) was a Unitarian minister and writer.

Hardy, Simon (pp. 83, 100, 102) is Senior Lecturer in Biology at the University of York and a member of Saint Saviourgate Unitarian Chapel.

Hawkins, Peter (pp. 26, 37, 112, 165) is the Chair of the Bath Consultancy Group, and a member of the Bath Unitarian Fellowship.

Hayhurst, Christine (p. 49) is Director of Public and Professional Affairs at the Institute of Management. She is a member of Meadrow Unitarian Chapel, Godalming, Surrey.

Henry Reinhardt, Aurelia (1877–1948) (p. 44) was elected the first woman moderator of the American Unitarian Association in 1940. She was a scholar, an educator, and a peace activist.

Hewett, Phillip (p. 44) was born in England and has served as minister to Unitarian churches in England and Canada. He is the author of numerous books.

Hill, Andrew (p. 24) is a retired Unitarian minister. He is the author of *Celebrating Life: a Book of Special Services for Use in the Unitarian Tradition.*

Hoehler, Judith L. (p. 94) is a Unitarian Universalist minister and former president of the Unitarian Universalist Christian Fellowship.

Holmes, John Haynes (1879–1964) (p. 90) was a Unitarian minister, socialist, and pacifist. He was a founder of the American Civil Liberties Union.

Hornby, Irene (p. 80) is a Unitarian in Lancashire.

Howe, Charles A. (pp. 17, 27, 82) is a Unitarian Universalist minister and historian, and author of many publications on Unitarian and Universalist history.

Howe, Julia Ward (1819–1910) (p. 108) was a poet, essayist, and reformer. She worked for the abolition of slavery, women's rights, and peace.

Hunter, Edith (p. 129) is a Unitarian Universalist religious educator.

Ingersoll, Robert G. (1833–1899) (p. 142) was an American political leader, attorney, orator, and agnostic.

Jefferson, Thomas (1743–1826) (pp. 88, 125) was the third president of the United States of America. He was the principal author of the American Declaration of Independence and the Bill for Establishing Religious Freedom in Virginia, establishing the principle of the separation of church and state in American politics. Born an Anglican, he never joined a Unitarian church but attended them while visiting Joseph Priestley in Pennsylvania. His own religious views were deistic and Unitarian.

Johnson, Raymond B. is a Unitarian Universalist minister.

Jones, Elizabeth M. (p. 133) is Director of Religious Education at the First Unitarian Universalist Church of San Diego, California.

Jones, Paula Cole (p. 173) is a management consultant and lifelong member of All Souls Church, Unitarian, in Washington, DC. She is a former president of DRUUMM (Diverse and Revolutionary Unitarian Universalist Multicultural Ministries).

Kendrick, Stephen (pp. 13, 149, 154) is the senior minister of First Church in Boston and author of *A Faith People Make.*

Kerr, Celia (pp. 79, 81) is a past president of the General Assembly of Unitarian and Free Christian Churches.

Killam, Robert (p. 95) was a Unitarian Universalist minister. He died in 1965.

Klees, Eileen M. (p. 60) is a member of Beverly Unitarian Church in Chicago.

Larsen, Tony (p. 69) is minister of Olympia Brown Unitarian Universalist Church in Racine, Wisconsin.

Lingwood, Stephen (pp. 30, 32, 37) is a Unitarian ministry student, due to complete his studies in 2008.

Longfellow, Henry Wadsworth (1807–1882) (p. 164) was a Unitarian poet.

Marshall, George N. (pp. 89, 121, 133, 137, 161) was a Unitarian minister and author of numerous books. He died in 1993.

Martineau, Harriet (1802–1876) (p. 153) was a journalist, novelist, and feminist. Her views on women's rights, slavery, and religion made her a controversial figure.

Martineau, James (1805–1900) (pp. 77, 135) was the most prominent figure in nineteenth-century British Unitarianism. A minister, theologian, and philosopher, he argued that the ultimate source of authority in religion is not the Bible but reason and conscience.

Mason, Helen (p. 145) is a lifelong Unitarian.

McClelland, Anne (p. 48) is a retired Unitarian minister and past president of the General Assembly of Unitarian and Free Christian Churches.

McNeile, Tony (p. 115) is a retired Unitarian minister and President of the National Unitarian Fellowship.

McTigue, Kathleen (p. 152) is senior minister of the Unitarian Society of New Haven, Connecticut.

Millard, Kay (pp. 1, 40) is the secretary of the Hibbert Trust and a member of Bath Unitarian Fellowship.

Monk, David (p. 138) is minister of Hindley Unitarian Chapel, Lancashire, a pastoral counsellor, meditation teacher, and leader of the Meditational Fellowship.

Morales, Peter (p. 72) is senior minister of Jefferson Unitarian Church, Golden, Colorado.

Morel Sullivan, Melanie is minister of the Unitarian Universalist Church in Cherry Hill, New Jersey.

Morrison-Reed, Mark (p. 38) is a Unitarian minister and a past president of the Canadian Unitarian Council.

Muir, Fredric John (pp. 30, 166) is minister of the Unitarian Universalist Church of Annapolis, Maryland, USA.

Murray, John (1741–1815) (p. 52) is considered the father of American Universalism. After the death of his family and persecution for his religious beliefs in England, he sailed to America to start a new life. He preached the Universalist Gospel all over America.

Newlin Leaming, Marjorie (p. 91) is a Unitarian Universalist minister and author of *Feminism from the Pulpit*.

Oelberg, Sarah (p. 64) is minister of the Nora Church Unitarian Universalist in Hanska, Minnesota and the Unitarian Universalist Fellowship in Mankato.

Oliver, Gordon (p. 55) is the minister of Cape Town Unitarian Church, South Africa, a former mayor of Cape Town, and the President of the International Council of Unitarians and Universalists.

Owen-Towle, Tom (pp. 18, 29, 31, 35, 77, 118, 124, 143, 152, 168, 170, 171) is a Unitarian Universalist minister and author of numerous books, including *Freethinking Mystics with Hands: Exploring the Heart of Unitarian Universalism*.

Paine, Thomas (1737–1809) (p. 128) was an English-born American radical writer. His ideas were influential in bringing about the American Revolution.

Parker, Theodore (1810–1860) (pp. 15, 60, 113, 158, 165, 170) was a Unitarian minister and Transcendentalist in Boston. A controversial figure, he worked for the abolition of slavery.

Pauling, Linus (1901–1994) (pp. 103, 110) was a scientist and campaigner against nuclear weapons. He won two Nobel Prizes, one for chemistry, and one for peace. He often gave talks at the Unitarian churches in Los Angeles and Pasadena.

Paxton, George (pp. 107, 109, 165, 169) is a former medical physicist and member of Glasgow Unitarian Church. He edits *The Gandhi Way*, the newsletter of the Gandhi Foundation.

Payne, Thomas (1942–2001) (p. 144) was a Unitarian Universalist minister.

Peart, Ann (pp. 83, 87, 93, 154, 156, 158) is a Unitarian minister and Principal of the Unitarian College in Manchester.

Peresluha   Elaine Beth (p. 148) is currently serving as interim minister of the Unitarian Universalist Fellowship in Wilmington, North Carolina.

Perkins, Palfrey (1883–1976) (p. 112) was an American Unitarian minister.

von Petzold, Gertrude (1876–1947) (pp. 32, 58, 79, 134, 168) was born in East Prussia but later moved to Britain and became the first female minister in England, when she became minister of the Free Christian Unitarian Church in Leicester in 1904.

Phillips, Roy D. (p. 118) is a Unitarian Universalist minister.

Pickett, O. Eugene (p. 17) was the fourth president of the Unitarian Universalist Association from 1979 to 1985.

Pierce, Ulysses G. B. (1865–1943) (p. 130) was a Unitarian minister who served forty years as pastor of All Souls' Church in Washington, DC.

Priestley, Joseph (1733–1804) (pp. 20, 28, 174) was one of the founders of Unitarianism in Britain. He was an influential minister, theologian, and scientist. In 1794 a mob burned down his home and laboratory in Birmingham, objecting to his support for the principles of the French Revolution. This eventually led to his emigration to Pennsylvania, where he died.

Pritchatt, Derrick (p. 101) is a retired lecturer in behavioural psychology and a member of Mill Hill Unitarian Chapel, Leeds.

Quest, Penny (pp. 114, 123, 136) is a British Unitarian and poet.

Ramage, Stephanie (p. 139) is a member of King Edward's Street Unitarian Chapel, Macclesfield.

Reed, Clifford Martin (usually known as **Cliff**) (pp. 56, 84, 94, 97, 98, 104, 107, 132, 151, 155, 172) is a Unitarian minister in Suffolk and a past president of the General Assembly of Unitarian and Free Christian Churches.

Reese, Curtis W. (1887–1961) (pp. 30, 104, 121) was a Unitarian minister, humanist, educator, social activist, and journalist. Originally a Southern Baptist minister, he became minister of a Unitarian church in 1913.

Reeves, Gene (p. 174) is former Dean of Meadville Lombard Theological School. He is a process philosopher and Buddhist.

Robinson, James A. (p. 125) is an American Unitarian Universalist.

Ruston, Alan (p. 76) is a Unitarian historian and past president of the General Assembly of Unitarian and Free Christian Churches.

Schulman, J. Frank (1927–2006) (pp. 91, 128) was a Unitarian minister who served churches in England and the United States. He was a historian and author of numerous books.

Schulz, William F. (p.13) was the fifth president of the Unitarian Universalist Association from 1985 to 1993. He served as executive director of Amnesty International USA from 1994 to 2006.

Schweitzer, Albert (1875–1965) (pp. 20, 22, 86, 154) was a German theologian, philosopher, musician, doctor and missionary. He was a member of the Unitarian Church of Cape Town, South Africa. His development of the 'ethic of reverence for life' has been influential in Unitarian thought.

Scott, Clinton Lee (1887–1985) (pp. 17, 42) was a Universalist minister, humanist, pacifist, social activist, and one of the architects of the merger between the Unitarians and Universalists.

Seon, Yvonne p.12) is an educator and Unitarian Universalist minister. She has pioneered the development of African American Studies curricula in American universities. In 1981 she became the first African American woman to be appointed as a Unitarian Universalist parish minister.

Servetus, Michael (c.1511–1553) (pp. 134, 174) was a theologian, physician, and martyr. A Spaniard, he travelled throughout Europe, debating with Protestant reformers and publishing his own work. For his writings against the doctrine of the Trinity, original sin, and child baptism, he was burned at the stake in John Calvin's Geneva in 1553.

Sienes, Rebecca Quimada (p. 54) is a Unitarian Universalist minister in the Philippines.

Sinkford, William G. (pp. 106, 141) is the seventh president, and the first African American president, of the Unitarian Universalist Association.

Skinner, Clarence (1881–1949) (p. 175) was the probably the most influential Universalist minister in the first half of the twentieth century. He was an educator, pacifist, socialist, and founder of the Community Church of Boston.

Smith, Betty (p. 60) is a Unitarian lay pastor and a member of Kendal Unitarian Chapel, Cumbria.

Smith, Matthew (p. 20) is a former Information Officer at Unitarian headquarters in London.

Socinus, Faustus (1539–1604) (p. 94) was born in Italy, but his anti-Trinitarian ideas were best received when he moved to Poland. Although officially called the Minor Reformed Church of Poland, the movement after his death is usually referred to as Socinianism. Socinian ideas and publications, including the Racovian Catechism, were influential in the development of English Unitarianism.

Spencer, Leon (p. 72) is Associate Professor and Coordinator of the Community Counseling Graduate Program in the Leadership Technology and Human Development Department at Georgia Southern University. He is a member of Statesboro Unitarian Universalist Fellowship, Georgia.

Stevenson, Adlai (1900–1965) (p. 27) was an American politician and diplomat. He was Governor of Illinois and ran twice for the presidency of the United States.

Stowe, Emily Howard Jennings (1831–1903) (p. 167) was a teacher, physician, and suffragist in Canada. Originally a Quaker, she later became a member of the Toronto Unitarian Church and was also involved in the Theosophical Society.

Streng, Frederick J. (1933–1993) (p. 36) was a professor of world religions, particularly Buddhist–Christian studies.

Sullivan, Melanie Morel (Rev. Melanie Morel Ensminger) (p. 65) is a Unitarian Universalist minister.

Tavkar, Ingrid (pp. 14, 85) worked for many years as the Social Responsibility Officer at the Unitarian headquarters in London.

Thandeka (pp. 41, 162, 168) is Senior Research Professor of Theology at Meadville Lombard Theological School in Chicago, and President of the Center for Community Values.

Thoreau, Henry David (1817–1862) (pp. 115, 116, 168) was an author, environmentalist, Transcendentalist, and philosopher. His most important works were *Walden* and *Civil Disobedience,* a book which influenced Leo Tolstoy, Mahondas Gandhi, and Martin Luther King.

Tinker, Sarah (pp. 25, 47, 130, 136) is the minister of Essex Unitarian Church, Kensington, London.

Trapp, Jacob (1899–1992) (p. 44) was a Unitarian Universalist minister.

Walker, Frank (pp. 15, 41) was the minister to the Cambridge Unitarian Church from 1976 until his retirement in 2000.

Wenzel, H. G. (p. 43) is an American Unitarian Universalist.

Wesley, Alice Blair (p. 23) is a Unitarian Universalist minister and author of *Our Covenant*.

Weston, Robert T. (p. 128) was a Unitarian minister in the USA in the twentieth century.

Whittemore, Thomas (1800–1861) (p. 153) was a historian and editor of Universalist publications.

Williams, David (p. 100) is the Emeritus Perren Professor of Astronomy at University College London and a Unitarian lay preacher.

Williams, Jane (pp. 112, 146) is a doctor of medicine and former president of the General Assembly of Unitarian and Free Christian Churches.

Williams, L. Griswold (p.13) was a Universalist minister in the first half of the twentieth century.

Winthrop, Katharine (p. 81) is a Unitarian Universalist minister.

Wollstonecraft, Mary (1759–1797) (p. 170) is often described as the first feminist. Her most important publication was *A Vindication of the Rights of Woman*. She was a member of Newington Green Unitarian Chapel, London.

Woolley, Celia Parker (1848–1918) (p.16) was a Unitarian minister, social-justice activist, and prolific writer. She worked mainly in Illinois.

York, Sarah (pp. 116, 125) is a Unitarian Universalist minister and author.

Notes

1   Cliff Reed, Peter Sampson, and Matthew F. Smith, leaflet: *A Faith Worth Thinking About* (London: General Assembly of Unitarian and Free Christian Churches).

2   Kay Millard, "Unitarian fellowship and the development of community" in *Prospects for the Unitarian Movement*, ed. Matthew F. Smith (London: Lindsey Press, 2002), p.128.

3   Art Lester, ed. Matthew Smith, leaflet: *The Flaming Chalice: Unitarian Symbol* (London: General Assembly of Unitarian and Free Christian Churches, 1994).

4   Christine Hayhurst, "Making vision work" in *Prospects for the Unitarian Movement*, ed. Matthew F. Smith (London: Lindsey Press, 2002), p.48.

5   Mel Hoover and Jacqui James, eds., pamphlet: *Soulful Journeys: The Faith of African American Unitarian Universalists* (Boston: Unitarian Universalist Association); reprinted with the permission of the UUA.

6   Francis David, adapted by Richard Fewkes, "God Is One", in *Singing the Living Tradition* (Boston: Unitarian Universalist Association, 1993), reading 566; by permission of Richard Fewkes.

7   *Singing the Living Tradition* (Boston: Unitarian Universalist Association, 1993), reading 459; reprinted with the permission of the author.

8   *Ibid.*, reading 471.

9   John A. Buehrens and Forrest Church, *A Chosen Faith: An Introduction to Unitarian Universalism* (Boston: Beacon Press, 1998), 211-212; by permission of the publisher.

10   *Unitarian Views of Human Nature* (leaflet) (London: General Assembly of Unitarian and Free Christian Churches).

11   Olympia Brown, "The Opening Doors", sermon preached in Universalist Church, Racine, Wisconsin, September 12, 1920, in *Standing Before Us: Unitarian Universalist Women and Social Reform, 1776 – 1936*, ed. Dorothy May Emerson (Boston: Skinner House Books, 2000), pp.465–6.

12   Cambridge Unitarian Church website (www.cam.net.uk/home/unitarian/leaflet.htm), accessed 11/3/05; reprinted with the permission of the author.

13   *Singing the Living Tradition* (Boston: Unitarian Universalist Association, 1993), reading 683.

14   Website of the Midland Union of Unitarian and Free Christian Churches (www.midlandunion.org.uk/why.html), accessed 11/3/05; reprinted by permission of the Midland Union.

15   Celia Parker Woolley, "The Ideal Unitarian Church" , from a paper read at Western Unitarian Conference, Chicago, May 16, 1889, in *Standing Before Us: Unitarian Universalist Women and Social Reform, 1776 – 1936*, ed. Dorothy May Emerson (Boston: Skinner House Books, 2000), pp. 486, 488.

16 Charles A. Howe, For *Faith and Freedom: A Short History of Unitarianism in Europe* (Boston: Skinner House Books, 1997), p.186; by permission of the publisher.

17 Tom Owen-Towle, *Freethinking Mystics With Hands: Exploring the Heart of Unitarian Universalism* (Boston: Skinner House Books, 1998), p.72; by permission of Tom Owen-Towle.

18 *Wayside Community Pulpit Series 6* (Boston: Unitarian Universalist Association, 1997) accessed 23/03/05 through the UUA Bookstore website (www.uua.org/bookstore/product_info.php?cPath=1&products_id=926).

19 Tom Owen-Towle, *Freethinking Mystics With Hands: Exploring the Heart of Unitarian Universalism* (Boston: Skinner House Books, 1998), p.7; reprinted with the permission of Tom Owen-Towle.

20 *Ibid.,* pp. 7, 81; by permission of the author.

21 Forrest Church, ed., *Without Apology: Collected Meditations on Liberal Religion by A. Powell Davies,* (Boston: Skinner House Books, 1998), p.16; reprinted by permission of the publisher.

22 Susan B. Anthony, "Woman's Rights and Wrongs", notes for speech, 1854, in *Standing Before Us: Unitarian Universalist Women and Social Reform, 1776 – 1936,* ed. Dorothy May Emerson (Boston: Skinner House Books, 2000), p.43.

23 *Unitarian Views of Jesus* (leaflet) (London: General Assembly of Unitarian and Free Christian Churches).

24 The Hibbert Assembly website (www.hibbert-assembly.org.uk/Priestley/sayings.htm), accessed 31/03/05.

25 George N. Marshall, *Challenge of a Liberal Faith,* 3rd ed. (Boston: Skinner House Books, 1991), pp. 42-43; reprinted with the permission of the publisher.

26 William Ellery Channing, "The free mind" in *Singing the Living Tradition* (Boston: Unitarian Universalist Association, 1993), reading 592.

27 George N. Marshall, *Challenge of a Liberal Faith,* 3rd ed. (Boston: Skinner House Books, 1991), p.43; reprinted by permission of the publisher.

28 James Luther Adams, *The Prophethood of All Believers* (Boston: Beacon Press, 1986), p.48; reprinted by permission of the publisher.

29 Brenda Wong, ed., *Quotations from the Wayside* (Boston: Skinner House Books, 1999), p.58; reprinted by permission of the publisher.

30 *Ibid.,* p.78; by permission of the publisher.

31 Imre Gellérd, *A History of Transylvanian Unitarianism through Four Centuries of Sermons,* trans. Judit Gellérd (Chico, CA: Uniquest, 1999), p.47; reprinted with the permission of the literary executors of Imre Gellérd .

32 Tom Owen-Towle, *Freethinking Mystics With Hands: Exploring the Heart of Unitarian Universalism* (Boston: Skinner House Books, 1998), p.23; by permission of Tom Owen-Towle.

33 Internet discussion, "Fuuse", reprinted by permission of the author.

34 *What Unitarians Mean By Tolerance* (leaflet) (London: General Assembly of Unitarian and Free Christian Churches, 1998).

35 *Ibid.*

36 *Ibid.*

37 Peter Hawkins, "Post-modernism and religion" in *Unitarian Perspectives on Contemporary Religious Thought*, ed. George D. Chryssides (London: Lindsey Press, 1999), p.39.

38 Charles A. Howe, *For Faith and Freedom: A Short History of Unitarianism in Europe* (Boston: Skinner House Books, 1997), p.187; by permission of the publisher.

39 John A. Buehrens and Forrest Church, *A Chosen Faith: An Introduction to Unitarian Universalism* (Boston: Beacon Press, 1998), p.81; by permission of the publisher.

40 Christine Hayhurst, "Making vision work", in *Prospects for the Unitarian Movement*, ed. Matthew F. Smith (London: Lindsey Press, 2002), p.46.

41 The Hibbert Assembly website (www.hibbert-assembly.org.uk/Priestley/sermons.htm), accessed 13/2/05.

42 Brenda Wong, ed., *Quotations from the Wayside* (Boston: Skinner House Books, 1999), p.31.

43 John Clifford, "A Universalist Sense of Ministry", General Assembly Anniversary Sermon, April 2003, Unitarian GA website (www.unitarian.org.uk/anniv_serm003.htm), accessed 30/1/05; reprinted by permission of the author.

44 The Commission on Appraisal of the Unitarian Universalist Association, *Interdependence: Renewing Congregational Polity* (Boston: Unitarian Universalist Association, 1997), p.2; by permission of the UUA.

45 Marjorie Bowens-Wheatley, "A litany of restoration", in *Singing the Living Tradition* (Boston: Unitarian Universalist Association, 1993), reading 576; by permission of the estate of Marjorie Bowens-Wheatley.

46 Tom Owen-Towle, *Freethinking Mystics With Hands: Exploring the Heart of Unitarian Universalism* (Boston: Skinner House Books, 1998), p.19; by permission of the author.

47 Curtis W. Reese, "The content of present-day religious liberalism" (1920) in *The Epic of Unitarianism: Original Writings from the History of Liberal Religion*, ed. David B. Parke (Boston: Starr King Press, 1957), p.136; reprinted by permission of Skinner House Books.

48 Written for this volume.

49 Fredrick John Muir, *Maglipay Universalist: A History of the Unitarian Universalist Church of the Philippines* (2001), p.83; with the permission of the author.

50 Matthew 22: 37 – 40, *New Revised Standard Version of the Bible*.

51 Nelson Simonson and John Morgan, "George de Benneville: Universalist mystic", *UU World*, May/June 2003 (www.uuworld.org/2003/03/lookingback.html), accessed 27/03/05.

52 Tom Owen-Towle, *Freethinking Mystics With Hands: Exploring the Heart of Unitarian Universalism* (Boston: Skinner House Books, 1998), p.91; by permission of the author.

53 Forrest Church, ed., *Without Apology: Collected Meditations on Liberal Religion by A. Powell Davies* (Boston: Skinner House Books, 1998), p.32; by permission of the publisher.

54 John Clifford, "A Universalist Sense of Ministry" , GA Anniversary Sermon, April 2003, Unitarian GA website (www.unitarian.org.uk/anniv_serm003.htm); accessed 30/1/05; reprinted by permission of the author.

55 Readings from "The Higher Life" (1908), three sermons by Gertrude von Petzold from the Hibbert Assembly website (www.hibbert-assembly.org.uk/womenswork/extracts.htm) accessed 28/2/05.

56 Written for this volume.

57 Elizabeth Blackwell, "The Influence of Women in the Profession of Medicine", lecture at opening of winter session, London School of Medicine for Women, October 1889, in *Standing Before Us: Unitarian Universalist Women and Social Reform, 1776 – 1936*, ed. Dorothy May Emerson (Boston: Skinner House Books, 2000), p.261.

58 Mel Hoover and Jacqui James, eds., pamphlet: *Soulful Journeys: The Faith of African American Unitarian Universalists* (Boston: Unitarian Universalist Association); by permission of the UUA.

59 Bill Darlison, "Encouraging congregational growth" in *Prospects for the Unitarian Movement*, ed. Matthew F. Smith, (London: Lindsey Press, 2002), p.109.

60 Tom Owen-Towle, *Freethinking Mystics With Hands: Exploring the Heart of Unitarian Universalism* (Boston: Skinner House Books, 1998), p.64; by permission of the author.

61 Tom Owen-Towle, *The Gospel of Universalism: Hope, Courage, and the Love of God* (Boston: Skinner House Books, 1993), p.32; by permission of the publisher.

62 John A. Buehrens and Forrest Church, *A Chosen Faith: An Introduction to Unitarian Universalism* (Boston: Beacon Press, 1998), p.97; by permission of the publisher.

63 Brenda Wong, ed., *Quotations from the Wayside* (Boston: Skinner House Books, 1999), p.70; by permission of the publisher.

64 Peter Hawkins, "Post-modernism and religion", in *Unitarian Perspectives on Contemporary Religious Thought*, ed. George D. Chryssides (London: Lindsey Press, 1999), p.40.

65 "Unitarian Futures" email discussion group, 6/10/04.

66 Mark Morrison-Reed, "The task of the religious community" , in *Singing the Living Tradition* (Boston: Unitarian Universalist Association, 1993), reading 580; by permission of the author.

67 John Buehrens, "Blessed are those", in *Singing the Living Tradition* (Boston: Unitarian Universalist Association, 1993), reading 728; by permission of the author.

68 Kay Millard, "Unitarian fellowship and the development of community", in *Prospects for the Unitarian Movement,* ed. Matthew F. Smith (London: Lindsey Press, 2002), pp. 123-4.

69 Cambridge Unitarian Church website (www.cam.net.uk/home/unitarian/leaflet.htm);accessed 23/03/05; reprinted with the permission of the author

70 Website of the Midland Union of Unitarian and Free Christian Churches (www.midlandunion.org.uk/why.html), accessed 23/03/05; by permission of the MU.

71 Fredric John Muir, *A Reason For Hope: Liberation Theology Confronts A Liberal Faith*, (Carmel, CA: Sunflower Ink, 1994), pp. 63–4; by permission of the publisher.

72 George Kimmich Beach, *Transforming Liberalism: The Theology of James Luther Adams* (Boston: Skinner House Books, 2005), pp.105–6; by permission of the publisher.

73 James Luther Adams, *The Prophethood of All Believers* (Boston: Beacon Press, 1986), p.59; by permission of the publisher.

74 Clinton Lee Scott, "Prophets", in *Singing The Living Tradition* (Boston: Unitarian Universalist Association, 1993), reading 565; by permission of the publisher.

75 John A. Buehrens and Forrest Church, *A Chosen Faith: An Introduction to Unitarian Universalism*, (Boston: Beacon Press, 1998), p.41; by permission of the publisher.

76 *Ibid.*, p.56; by permission of the publisher.

77 Aurelia Isabel Henry Reinhardt, "Worship: its fundamental place in liberal religion", From Report of the Commission on Appraisal, American Unitarian Association, 1936, in *Standing Before Us: Unitarian Universalist Women and Social Reform, 1776 – 1936*, ed. Dorothy May Emerson (Boston: Skinner House Books, 2000), p.562.

78 John A. Buehrens and Forrest Church, *A Chosen Faith: An Introduction to Unitarian Universalism* (Boston: Beacon Press, 1998), p.134; by permission of the publisher.

79 Jacob Trapp, "To worship", in *Singing the Living Tradition* (Boston: Unitarian Universalist Association, 1993), reading 441.

80 Anna Laetitia Aikin Barbauld, "Mrs. Barbauld's thoughts on public worship", in *Standing Before Us: Unitarian Universalist Women and Social Reform, 1776–1936*, ed. Dorothy May Emerson (Boston: Skinner House Books, 2000), p.477.

81 Michaela von Britzke, "Fostering spiritual growth in our Unitarian communities", in *Prospects for the Unitarian Movement*, ed. Matthew F. Smith (London: Lindsey Press, 2002), pp. 99–100.

82 Bill Darlison, "Encouraging congregational growth", *Prospects for the Unitarian Movement*, ed. Matthew F. Smith (London: Lindsey Press, 2002), pp. 111–12.

83 "Religious education programmes for all ages" (Unitarian General Assembly website, 2000), quoted by Melanie Prideaux in "A Unitarian perspective on school education", *Unitarian Perspectives on Contemporary Social Issues*, ed. George Chryssides (London: Lindsey Press, 2003), p.55.

84 Sarah Tinker, "The future for religious education in the Unitarian movement", *Prospects for the Unitarian Movement*, ed. Matthew F. Smith (London: Lindsey Press, 2002), p.44.

85 Brenda Wong, ed., *Quotations from the Wayside* (Boston: Skinner House Books, 1999), p.57.

86 Anne McClelland, "Creation Spirituality and social issues", *Unitarian Perspectives on Contemporary Social Issues*, ed. George Chryssides (London: Lindsey Press, 2003), p.19.

87 Christine Hayhurst, "Making vision work", *Prospects for the Unitarian Movement*, ed. Matthew F. Smith (London: Lindsey Press, 2002), p.49.

88 Personal communication with the editor, 24/11/04.

89 The Commission on Appraisal of the Unitarian Universalist Association, *Interdependence: Renewing Congregational Polity* (Boston: Unitarian Universalist Association, 1997), p.169; by permission of the UUA.

90 George Chryssides, *The Elements of Unitarianism* (Shaftesbury, Dorset: Element Books, 1998), p.116; by permission of the author.

91 John Clifford, "A Universalist Sense of Ministry", GA Anniversary Sermon, April 2003, Unitarian GA website (www.unitarian.org.uk/anniv_serm003.htm); accessed 30/1/05; by permission of the author.

92 Christine Hayhurst, "Making vision work", *Prospects for the Unitarian Movement*, ed. Matthew F. Smith (London: Lindsey Press, 2002), p.46.

93 Tom Owen-Towle, *The Gospel of Universalism: Hope, Courage, and the Love of God* (Boston: Skinner House Books, 1993), p. v.

94 International Council of Unitarians and Universalists (www.icuu.net/aboutus/index.html), accessed 23/03/05.

95 *Singing the Living Tradition* (Boston: Unitarian Universalist Association, 1993), reading 516.

96 Fredrick John Muir, *Maglipay Universalist: A History of the Unitarian Universalist Church of the Philippines* (2001), p.45; by permission of Fredrick John Muir.

97 Norbert F. Capek, "Consecration of the Flowers", *Singing the Living Tradition* (Boston: Unitarian Universalist Association, 1993), reading 724.

98 Imre Gellérd, *A History of Transylvanian Unitarianism Through Four Centuries of Sermons*, trans. Judit Gellérd (Chico, CA: Uniquest, 1999), p.75; by permission of the estate of Imre Gellérd .

99 Gordon Oliver, "Cape Town calling", *The Inquirer*, 31 May 2003, p. 6; by permission of the Editor.

100 George Chryssides, *The Elements of Unitarianism* (Shaftesbury, Dorset: Element Books, 1998), pp. 79–80; by permission of the author.

101 *Unitarian Views of Jesus* (leaflet) (London: General Assembly of Unitarian and Free Christian Churches).

102 George N. Marshall, *Challenge of a Liberal Faith*, 3rd ed. (Boston: Skinner House Books, 1991), p.61; by permission of the publisher.

103 Matt Grant, "Clash of civilisations? A Unitarian Christian response", *The Unitarian Christian Herald*, No 55, Autumn 2004; by permission of the author.

104 George Chryssides, *The Elements of Unitarianism* (Shaftesbury, Dorset: Element Books, 1998), pp. 99-100; by permission of the author.

105 John Clifford, "A Universalist Sense of Ministry", GA Anniversary Sermon, April 2003, Unitarian GA website (www.unitarian.org.uk/anniv_serm003.htm), accessed 30/1/05; by permission of the author.

106 Readings from "The Higher Life" (1908), three sermons by Gertrude von Petzold, Hibbert Assembly website (www.hibbert-assembly.org.uk/womenswork/extracts.htm), accessed 28/2/05.

107 "Why I am a Christian among the Unitarian Universalists", Unitarian Universalist Christian Fellowship website (www.uua.org/uucf/whyiam.htm), accessed 22/11/04; reprinted by permission of the UUCF.

108 *Unitarian Views of Jesus* (leaflet) (London: General Assembly of Unitarian and Free Christian Churches).

109 Theodore Parker, "The transient and permanent in Christianity" (1841), in David B. Parke, *The Epic of Unitarianism: Original Writings from the History of Liberal Religion* (Boston: Starr King Press, 1957), pp. 113–14.

110 James Ishmael Ford, pamphlet: *The Faith of a Buddhist* (Boston: Unitarian Universalist Association); reprinted by permission of the UUA.

111 Sarah Oelberg, pamphlet: *The Faith of a Humanist* (Boston: Unitarian Universalist Association); reprinted by permission of the UUA.

112 The Midland Union of Unitarian and Free Christian Churches website, (www.midlandunion.org.uk/why.html), accessed 23/03/05; reprinted by permission of the MU.

113 Tom Owen-Towle, *Freethinking Mystics With Hands: Exploring the Heart of Unitarian Universalism* (Boston: Skinner House Books, 1998), p. 65; reprinted by permission of Tom Owen-Towle.

114 Rosemary Bray McNatt, pamphlet: *The Faith of a Theist* (Boston: Unitarian Universalist Association); reprinted by permission of the UUA.

115 Barbara L. Pescan, pamphlet: *Unitarian Universalism, A Religious Home for Bisexual, Gay, Lesbian, and Transgender People* (Boston: Unitarian Universalist Association); by permission of the UUA.

116 *Ibid.*

117 Scott W. Alexander, pamphlet: *Unitarian Universalism: A Welcoming Place for Bisexual, Gay, Lesbian, and Transgender People* (Boston: Unitarian Universalist Association); by permission of the UUA.

118 *Ibid.*

119 *What Unitarians Mean By Tolerance* (leaflet) (London: General Assembly of Unitarian and Free Christian Churches, 1998).

120 Lynn Dobbs, "Look to this day", in *Blessed Bi Spirit: Bisexual People of Faith* ed. Debra R. Kolodny (New York: Continuum, 2000); by permission of the publisher.

121 Mel Hoover and Jacqui James, eds., pamphlet: *Soulful Journeys: The Faith of African American Unitarian Universalists* (Boston: Unitarian Universalist Association); by permission of the UUA.

122 Ervin Barrios and Julio Noboa, eds., pamphlet: *Latino/Latina Spiritual Journeys* (Boston: Unitarian Universalist Association); by permission of the UUA.

123 Jane Aaronson, "Without Prejudice: Living with a Disability", keynote address to the General Assembly meetings in Edinburgh in 2003 (when the theme was "Removing Barriers, Unitarians Address Disability Issues"); reprinted with the permission of the author.

124 Brenda Wong, ed., *Quotations from the Wayside* (Boston: Skinner House Books, 1999), p.49; by permission of the publisher.

125 *Unitarian Views of Human Nature* (leaflet) (London: General Assembly of Unitarian and Free Christian Churches).

126 *Ibid.*

127 George N. Marshall, *Challenge of a Liberal Faith*, 3rd ed. (Boston: Skinner House Books, 1991), p.42.

128 Forrest Church, ed., *Without Apology: Collected Meditations on Liberal Religion by A. Powell Davies*, (Boston: Skinner House Books, 1998), p.14; reprinted by permission of the publisher.

129 James Martineau, "Three Stages of Unitarian Theology" (1869), in *The Epic of Unitarianism: Original Writings from the History of Liberal Religion*, ed. David B. Parke (Boston: Starr King Press, 1957), p.74.

130 Tom Owen-Towle, *Freethinking Mystics With Hands: Exploring the Heart of Unitarian Universalism* (Boston: Skinner House Books, 1998), pp. 48–9; by permission of the author.

131 Forrest Church, ed., *Without Apology: Collected Meditations on Liberal Religion by A. Powell Davies* (Boston: Skinner House Books, 1998), pp. 71, 73; by permission of the publisher.

132 Readings from "The Higher Life" (1908), three sermons by Gertrude von Petzold, from the Hibbert Assembly website (www.hibbert-assembly.org.uk/womenswork/extracts.htm), accessed 28/2/05.

133 Ingrid Tavkar, ed., leaflet: *Women in the Unitarian Movement* (London: General Assembly of Unitarian and Free Christian Churches).

134 *Ibid.*

135 *Ibid.*

136 *Ibid.*

137 Tom Owen-Towle, *Freethinking Mystics With Hands: Exploring the Heart of Unitarian Universalism* (Boston: Skinner House Books, 1998), p.47; by permission of Tom Owen-Towle.

138 Charles A. Howe, *For Faith and Freedom: A Short History of Unitarianism in Europe* (Boston: Skinner House Books, 1997), p.187; by permission of the publisher.

139 Simon Hardy, "Questions", in *Waiting to Be Discovered: Revealing Life's Hidden Possibilities*, eds. Johanna Boeke and Joy Croft (London: Unitarian General Assembly Worship Committee, 2003), pp. 6–7.

140 Matthew Smith, ed., leaflet: *Unitarian Views of Earth and Nature* (London: General Assembly of Unitarian and Free Christian Churches, 1994).

141 *Ibid.*

142 *Ibid.*

143 *Ibid.*

144 Albert Schweitzer, "The ethic of reverence for life", in *Civilization and Ethics*, ed. C.T. Campion, Unwin Books (London: Adam & Charles Black, 1967 ed.), pp. 214–22. Permission applied for.

145 Matthew Smith, ed., leaflet: *Unitarian Views of Earth and Nature* (London: General Assembly of Unitarian and Free Christian Churches, 1994).

146 J.A.C.F. Auer *et al.*, "A Humanist Manifesto" (1933) in *The Epic of Unitarianism: Original Writings from the History of Liberal Religion*, ed. David B. Parke (Boston: Starr King Press, 1957), p.140; by permission of Skinner House books.

147 Alistair Bate, "Discovering unity" in *Waiting to Be Discovered: Revealing life's hidden possibilities*, ed. Johanna Boeke and Joy Croft (London: Unitarian General Assembly Worship Committee, 2003), 21.

148 Thomas Jefferson, a letter to his nephew (1787) in *The Epic of Unitarianism: Original Writings from the History of Liberal Religion*, ed. David B. Parke (Boston: Starr King Press, 1957), pp. 66–7.

149 William Ellery Channing, "Unitarian Christianity", *ibid.*, pp. 90–92.

150 Imre Gellérd, *A History of Transylvanian Unitarianism Through Four Centuries of Sermons*, trans. Judit Gellérd (Chico, CA: Uniquest, 1999), pp. 45–6; by permission of the author's estate.

151 George N. Marshall, *Challenge of a Liberal Faith*, 3rd ed. (Boston: Skinner House Books, 1991), p. 120; by permission of the publisher.

152 *Ibid.*, p. 129.

153 *Ibid.*, pp. 134–5.

154 John Biddle, "Confession of faith" (1648), in *The Epic of Unitarianism: Original Writings from the History of Liberal Religion* ed. David B. Parke (Boston: Starr King Press, 1957), p.31.

155 Ralph Waldo Emerson (1837), *ibid.*, p.105.

156 James Luther Adams, *The Prophethood of All Believers* (Boston: Beacon Press, 1986), p.49; by permission of the publisher.

157 Brenda Wong, ed., *Quotations from the Wayside* (Boston: Skinner House Books, 1999), p.44; by permission of the publisher.

158 *Ibid.*, p.45; by permission of the publisher.

159 Johanna Boeke, "Goodbye to God the Father", in *Waiting to Be Discovered: Revealing Life's Hidden Possibilities*, eds. Johanna Boeke and Joy Croft (London: Unitarian General Assembly Worship Committee, 2003), p.20.

160 Lena Cockroft, "Have I discovered God?", *ibid.*, pp. 22–3.

161 Forrest Church, ed., *Without Apology: Collected Meditations on Liberal Religion by A. Powell Davies*, (Boston: Skinner House Books, 1998), p.79; by permission of the publisher.

162 Ann Peart, "Forgotten prophets: Unitarian women and religion", in *Unitarian Perspectives on Contemporary Religious Thought*, ed. George D. Chryssides (London: Lindsey Press, 1999), p.73.

163 Dorothy May Emerson, ed., *Standing Before Us: Unitarian Universalist Women and Social Reform, 1776–1936* (Boston: Skinner House Books, 2000), p.66.

164 Faustus Socinus *et al.*, "Racovian Catechism" (1605) in *The Epic of Unitarianism: Original Writings from the History of Liberal Religion*, ed. David B. Parke (Boston: Starr King Press, 1957), pp. 26–7.

165 John A. Buehrens and Forrest Church, *A Chosen Faith: An Introduction to Unitarian Universalism* (Boston: Beacon Press, 1998), pp. 119–120; by permission of the publisher.

166 *Unitarian Views of Jesus* (leaflet) (London: General Assembly of Unitarian and Free Christian Churches).

167 George N. Marshall, *Challenge of a Liberal Faith*, 3rd ed. (Boston: Skinner House Books, 1991), p.140; by permission of the publisher.

168 John Biddle, "Confession of faith" (1648) in *The Epic of Unitarianism: Original Writings from the History of Liberal Religion* ed. David B. Parke (Boston: Starr King Press, 1957), p.32.

169 Ralph Waldo Emerson, "Divinity School Address" (1838) in *The Epic of Unitarianism: Original Writings from the History of Liberal Religion* ed. David B. Parke (Boston: Starr King Press, 1957), p.108.

170 Andrew Brown, "Is there a future for the Unitarian Christian tradition?" in *Prospects for the Unitarian Movement*, ed. Matthew F. Smith (London: Lindsey Press, 2002), pp.10, 11, 15.

171 Cliff Reed, *Unitarian? What's That?* (London: Lindsey Press, 1999); by permission of the author.

172 *Ibid.*; by permission of the author.

173 John A. Buehrens, *Understanding the Bible: An Introduction for Skeptics, Seekers, and Religious Liberals,* (Boston: Beacon Press, 2003), pp. 3–4; by permission of the publisher.

174 Brenda Wong, ed., *Quotations from the Wayside* (Boston: Skinner House Books, 1999), p.84.

175 Simon Hardy, "Science, religion, and culture" in *Unitarian Perspectives on Contemporary Social Issues,* ed. George Chryssides, (London: Lindsey Press, 2003), p.94.

176 David Williams, "Lessons From Joseph Priestley", Essex Hall Lecture, 2004, from the Unitarian GA website (www.unitarian.org.uk/lectures_ehl2004.htm), accessed 31/1/05; by permission of the author.

177 *Unitarian Views of Human Nature* (leaflet) (London: General Assembly of Unitarian and Free Christian Churches).

178 Simon Hardy, "Science, religion, and culture" in *Unitarian Perspectives on Contemporary Social Issues,* ed. George Chryssides (London: Lindsey Press, 2003), p.112.

179 Tony Cann and George Chryssides, "Unitarians and the Internet", in *Unitarian Perspectives on Contemporary Social Issues,* ed. George Chryssides (London: Lindsey Press, 2003), pp. 117, 120, 124.

180 Barbara Marinacci, ed., *Linus Pauling in His Own Words: Selected Writings, Speeches, and Interviews* (New York: Touchstone Books, 1995), p. 12; by permission of Simon & Schuster, Inc.

181 *Standing Before Us: Unitarian Universalist Women and Social Reform, 1776–1936,* ed. Dorothy May Emerson (Boston: Skinner House Books, 2000), p.52.

182 Cliff Reed, *Unitarian? What's That?* (London: Lindsey Press, 1999); by permission of the author.

183 Curtis W. Reese, "The content of present-day religious liberalism" (1920), in *The Epic of Unitarianism: Original Writings from the History of Liberal Religion,* ed. David B. Parke (Boston: Starr King Press, 1957), p.136; by permission of Skinner House Books.

184 Frances Power Cobbe, "To an audience of ladies", London, 1881, in *Standing Before Us: Unitarian Universalist Women and Social Reform, 1776–1936,* ed. Dorothy May Emerson (Boston: Skinner House Books, 2000), p.88.

185 J. Ronald Engel, "Liberal democracy and the fate of the Earth", in *Spirit and Nature: Why the Environment Is a Religious Issue,* eds. Steven C. Rockefeller and John C. Elder, (Boston: Beacon Press, 1992), pp. 64, 67, 69, 70, 78; by permission of the publisher.

186 William G. Sinkford, statement released by President of the Unitarian Universalist Association after the 2004 American Presidential election, 3 November 2004 (www.uua.org/president/041103.html), accessed 31/03/05; by permission of the UUA.

187 Cliff Reed, *Unitarian? What's That?* (London: Lindsey Press, 1999); by permission of the author.

188 George Paxton, "Can war be abolished?", in *Unitarian Perspectives on Contemporary Social Issues,* ed. George Chryssides (London: Lindsey Press, 2003), 77.

189 Julia Ward Howe, "Mother's Day Proclamation" in *Singing The Living Tradition,* (Boston: Unitarian Universalist Association, 1993), reading 573.

190 Olympia Brown, "Opening Doors", sermon preached in Universalist Church, Racine, Wisconsin, September 12, 1920, in *Standing Before Us: Unitarian Universalist Women and Social Reform, 1776–1936*, ed. Dorothy May Emerson (Boston: Skinner House Books, 2000), p.465.

191 *Unitarian Views of Human Nature* (leaflet) (London: General Assembly of Unitarian and Free Christian Churches).

192 Barbara Marinacci, ed., *Linus Pauling in His Own Words: Selected Writings, Speeches, and Interviews* (New York: Touchstone Books, 1995), pp. 184–6; by permission of Simon & Schuster, Inc.

193 Brenda Wong, ed., *Quotations from the Wayside* (Boston: Skinner House Books, 1999), p.35; by permission of the publisher.

194 Ingrid Tavkar, ed., leaflet: *Women in the Unitarian Movement* (London: General Assembly of Unitarian and Free Christian Churches).

195 Peter Hawkins, "Post-modernism and religion", in *Unitarian Perspectives on Contemporary Religious Thought*, ed. George D. Chryssides (London: Lindsey Press, 1999), p.41.

196 William Ellery Channing, "Unitarian Christianity" in *Three Prophets of Religious Liberalism: Channing, Emerson, Parker*, ed. Conrad Wright (Boston: Beacon Press, 1961), pp. 87–8.

197 Theodore Parker, "The transient and permanent in Christianity" (1841), in *The Epic of Unitarianism: Original Writings from the History of Liberal Religion*, ed. David B. Parke (Boston: Starr King Press, 1957), p.114.

198 Brenda Wong, ed., *Quotations from the Wayside* (Boston: Skinner House Books, 1999), p.70; by permission of the publisher.

199 Penny Quest, "Learning as we live", in *Waiting to Be Discovered: Revealing Life's Hidden Possibilities*, eds. Johanna Boeke and Joy Croft (London: Unitarian General Assembly Worship Committee, 2003), pp.34–5.

200 Brenda Wong, ed., *Quotations from the Wayside* (Boston: Skinner House Books, 1999), p.65.

201 Tony McNeile, the Newsletter of Bank Street Unitarian Chapel, Bolton; by permission of the author.

202 Sara Moores Campbell, "Give us the spirit of the child", in *Singing The Living Tradition* (Boston: Unitarian Universalist Association, 1993), reading 664; by permission of the author.

203 Henry David Thoreau, "To live deliberately", *ibid.*, reading 660.

204 Bill Darlison, sermon, "The Many-Splendoured Thing", from Dublin Unitarian Church website (www.unitarianchurchdublin.org/sermons/The%20Many-Splendoured%20Thing.htm), accessed 06/11/04; by permission of the author.

205 Brenda Wong, ed., *Quotations from the Wayside* (Boston: Skinner House Books, 1999), p.89; by permission of the publisher.

206 George N. Marshall, *Challenge of a Liberal Faith*, 3rd ed. (Boston: Skinner House Books, 1991), p.38.

207 Tom Owen-Towle, *Freethinking Mystics With Hands: Exploring the Heart of Unitarian Universalism* (Boston: Skinner House Books, 1998), p.24; by permission of the author.

208 Charles A. Howe, *For Faith and Freedom: A Short History of Unitarianism in Europe* (Boston: Skinner House Books, 1997), p.95.

209 Ralph Waldo Emerson (adapted), "These roses", in *Singing The Living Tradition* (Boston: Unitarian Universalist Association, 1993), reading 556.

210 James Luther Adams, "A faith for free men" (1946), in *The Epic of Unitarianism: Original Writings from the History of Liberal Religion*, ed. David B. Parke (Boston: Starr King Press, 1957), pp. 150–1; by permission of Skinner House Books.

211 Andrew Brown, "Is there a future for the Unitarian Christian tradition?" in *Prospects for the Unitarian Movement*, ed. Matthew F. Smith (London: Lindsey Press, 2002), p.9.

212 George N. Marshall, *Challenge of a Liberal Faith*, 3rd ed. (Boston: Skinner House Books, 1991), p. 17; by permission of the publisher.

213 *Ibid.*, pp. 19-20.

214 Joy Croft, "Soul music", in *Waiting to Be Discovered: Revealing Life's Hidden Possibilities*, eds. Johanna Boeke and Joy Croft (London: Unitarian General Assembly Worship Committee, 2003), pp. 10–11.

215 Penny Quest, "Each new morning", *ibid.*, p. 49.

216 Tom Owen-Towle, *Freethinking Mystics With Hands: Exploring the Heart of Unitarian Universalism* (Boston: Skinner House Books, 1998), p.7; by permission of the author.

217 Mel Hoover and Jacqui James, eds., pamphlet: *Soulful Journeys: The Faith of African American Unitarian Universalists* (Boston: Unitarian Universalist Association); by permission of the UUA.

218 *Wayside Community Pulpit Series 6* (Boston: Unitarian Universalist Association, 1997) accessed through the UUA Bookstore website (www.uua.org/bookstore/product_info.php?cPath=1&products_id=926) 23/03/05; by permission of the UUA.

219 *Singing The Living Tradition* (Boston: Unitarian Universalist Association, 1993), reading 701; by permission of the author.

220 Thomas Jefferson, a letter to his nephew (1787), in *The Epic of Unitarianism: Original Writings from the History of Liberal Religion*, ed. David B. Parke (Boston: Starr King Press, 1957), p.67.

221 *The Epistula Apostolorum*, verse 25, from *The Complete Jesus*, trans. and ed. by Ricky Alan Mayotte (South Rayalton, VT: Steerforth Press, 1998), p.131.

222 Sophia Lyon Fahs, "It matters what we believe", in *Singing The Living Tradition* (Boston: Unitarian Universalist Association, 1993), reading 657; by permission of the publisher.

223 John Hunt, *Daddy, Do You Believe In God?* (Alresford, Hampshire: O Books, 2001), p.353.

224 Brenda Wong, ed., *Quotations from the Wayside* (Boston: Skinner House Books, 1999), p. 35; by permission of the publisher.

225 Robert T. Weston, "Cherish your doubts", in *Singing The Living Tradition* (Boston: Unitarian Universalist Association, 1993), reading 650; by permission of the author's estate.

226 George N. Marshall, *Challenge of a Liberal Faith*, 3rd ed. (Boston: Skinner House Books, 1991), p.100.

227 James Luther Adams, *The Prophethood of All Believers* (Boston: Beacon Press, 1986), pp. 52–3; by permission of the publisher.

228 George N. Marshall, *Challenge of a Liberal Faith*, 3rd ed. (Boston: Skinner House Books, 1991), p.101; by permission of the publisher.

229 Forrest Church, ed., *Without Apology: Collected Meditations on Liberal Religion by A. Powell Davies* (Boston: Skinner House Books, 1998), pp. 65-6; by permission of the publisher.

230 Brenda Wong, ed., *Quotations from the Wayside* (Boston: Skinner House Books, 1999), p. 81; by permission of the publisher.

231 *Ibid.*, p.87.

232 Sarah Tinker, "The future for religious education in the Unitarian movement", in *Prospects for the Unitarian Movement*, ed. Matthew F. Smith (London: Lindsey Press, 2002), p.43.

233 Michaela von Britzke, "Fostering spiritual growth in our Unitarian communities", *ibid.*, p. 99.

234 Imre Gellérd, *A History of Transylvanian Unitarianism Through Four Centuries of Sermons*, trans. Judit Gellérd (Chico, CA: Uniquest, 1999), p.49; by permission of the author's estate.

235 Forrest Church, ed., *Without Apology: Collected Meditations on Liberal Religion by A. Powell Davies*, (Boston: Skinner House Books, 1998), pp. 13–14; by permission of the publisher.

236 Judit Gellérd, *Prisoner of Liberté: Story of a Transylvanian Martyr* (Chico, CA: Uniquest, 2003), p.2; by permission of the author's estate.

237 Cliff Reed, *Unitarian? What's That?* (London: Lindsey Press, 1999); by permission of the author.

238 George N. Marshall, *Challenge of a Liberal Faith*, 3rd ed. (Boston: Skinner House Books, 1991), p. 152; by permission of the publisher.

239 John A. Buehrens and Forrest Church, *A Chosen Faith: An Introduction to Unitarian Universalism*, (Boston: Beacon Press, 1998), p.18; by permission of the publisher.

240 Ralph Waldo Emerson, "The oversoul", in *Singing The Living Tradition* (Boston: Unitarian Universalist Association, 1993), reading 531.

241 Michael Servetus, "On the errors of the Trinity" (1531), in *The Epic of Unitarianism: Original Writings from the History of Liberal Religion*, ed. David B. Parke (Boston: Starr King Press, 1957), p.6.

242 Readings from "The Higher Life" (1908), three sermons by Gertrude von Petzold from the Hibbert Assembly website (www.hibbert-assembly.org.uk/womenswork/extracts.htm), accessed 28/2/05.

243 James Martineau, "Three stages of Unitarian theology" (1869) in *The Epic of Unitarianism: Original Writings from the History of Liberal Religion*, ed. David B. Parke (Boston: Starr King Press, 1957), pp. 75–6.

244 Website of Chorley Unitarian Chapel (www.users.waitrose.com/~hil/chorleychapel/pages/reflections1.htm), accessed 23/03/05.

245 Sarah Tinker, "The future for religious education in the Unitarian movement", in *Prospects for the Unitarian Movement*, ed. Matthew F. Smith (London: Lindsey Press, 2002), pp. 41–2.

246 Penny Quest, "Never a moment", in *Waiting to Be Discovered: Revealing Life's Hidden Possibilities*, eds. Johanna Boeke and Joy Croft (London: Unitarian General Assembly Worship Committee, 2003), p.17.

247 George N. Marshall, *Challenge of a Liberal Faith*, 3rd ed. (Boston: Skinner House Books, 1991), p.120; by permission of the publisher.

248 Brenda Wong, ed., *Quotations from the Wayside* (Boston: Skinner House Books, 1999), p. 83.

249 *Unitarian Views of Human Nature* (leaflet) (London: General Assembly of Unitarian and Free Christian Churches).

250 Brenda Wong, ed., *Quotations from the Wayside* (Boston: Skinner House Books, 1999), p.43; by permission of the publisher.

251 *Ibid.*, p.79; by permission of the publisher.

252 Stephanie Ramage, "Help me to pray", in *Waiting to Be Discovered: Revealing Life's Hidden Possibilities*, eds. Johanna Boeke and Joy Croft (London: Unitarian General Assembly Worship Committee, 2003), p.71.

253 Forrest Church, ed., *Without Apology: Collected Meditations on Liberal Religion by A. Powell Davies* (Boston: Skinner House Books, 1998), pp. 87–8; by permission of the publisher.

254 William G. Sinkford, "The Language of Faith", sermon preached at First Jefferson Unitarian Universalist Church, January 12, 2003; in *A Language of Reverence*, ed. Dean Grodzins (Chicago: Meadville Lombard Press, 2004), p.5; by permission of the publisher.

255 Ontario Consultants on Religious Tolerance website (www.religioustolerance.org/quotes7.htm), accessed 17/06/05.

256 Tom Owen-Towle, *The Gospel of Universalism: Hope, Courage, and the Love of God,* (Boston: Skinner House Books, 1993), p.24; by permission of the publisher.

257 George N. Marshall, *Challenge of a Liberal Faith*, 3rd ed. (Boston: Skinner House Books, 1991), p.61.

258 Brenda Wong, ed., *Quotations from the Wayside* (Boston: Skinner House Books, 1999), p.85.

259 "Winchester Profession" (1803) in *Universalism In America: A Documentary History of a Liberal Faith*, 3rd ed., ed. Ernest Cassara (Boston: Skinner House Books, 1997), p.110.

260 Anna Laetitia Aikin Barbauld, "Mrs. Barbauld's thoughts on public worship" in *Standing Before Us: Unitarian Universalist Women and Social Reform, 1776 – 1936*, ed. Dorothy May Emerson (Boston: Skinner House Books, 2000), p.479.

261 Tom Owen-Towle, *Freethinking Mystics With Hands: Exploring the Heart of Unitarian Universalism* (Boston: Skinner House Books, 1998), p.90; by permission of the author.

262 Mel Hoover and Jacqui James eds., pamphlet: *Soulful Journeys: The Faith of African American Unitarian Universalists* (Boston: Unitarian Universalist Association); by permission of the UUA.

263 Ingrid Tavkar, ed., leaflet: *Women in the Unitarian Movement* (London: General Assembly of Unitarian and Free Christian Churches).

264 *Ibid.*

265 James Luther Adams, *The Prophethood of All Believers* (Boston: Beacon Press, 1986), p.290; by permission of the publisher.

266 Elaine Beth Peresluha, "You Are Only Old Once", sermon delivered at the Unitarian Universalist Society Of Bangor, Maine, 19 May 2002. Accessed from the website of the Unitarian Universalist Society of Bangor (www.uubangor.org/sermon-May19,2002.htm) on 21/03/05; with the author's permission.

267 Stephen Kendrick, "Well Being and Being Well", sermon delivered at the First and Second Church in Boston, Massachusetts, 1 February 2004.; accessed from the website of First and Second Church (www.fscboston.org/sermons.php) on 06/03/05; by permission of the author.

268 Elizabeth Blackwell, "The Influence of Women in the Profession of Medicine", lecture at opening of the winter session, London School of Medicine for Women, October 1889, in *Standing Before Us: Unitarian Universalist Women and Social Reform, 1776 – 1936*, ed. Dorothy May Emerson (Boston: Skinner House Books, 2000), pp.256-7.

269 Cliff Reed, *Unitarian? What's That?* (London: Lindsey Press, 1999); by permission of the author.

270 Kathleen McTigue, "They are with us still" in *Singing The Living Tradition* (Boston: Unitarian Universalist Association, 1993), reading 721; by permission of the author.

271 Tom Owen-Towle, *Freethinking Mystics With Hands: Exploring the Heart of Unitarian Universalism* (Boston: Skinner House Books, 1998), p.94; by permission of the author.

272 George Chryssides, *The Elements of Unitarianism* (Shaftesbury, Dorset: Element Books, 1998), p. 60; by permission of the author.

273 Thomas Whittemore, "The Plain Guide to Universalism" (1840) in *Universalism in America: A Documentary History of a Liberal Faith*, 3rd ed., ed. Ernest Cassara (Boston, Skinner House Books, 1997), p. 136.

274 Harriet Martineau, *Autobiography Volume II* (Westmead, Farnborough, Hants., England: Gregg International Publishers, 1969) pp. 435, 437.

275 John A. Buehrens and Forrest Church, *A Chosen Faith: An Introduction to Unitarian Universalism*, (Boston: Beacon Press, 1998), p.18; by permission of the publisher.

276 Brenda Wong, ed., *Quotations from the Wayside* (Boston: Skinner House Books, 1999), p.87.

277 Ann Peart, "Of warmth and love and passion: Unitarians and (homo)sexuality", in *Unitarian Perspectives on Contemporary Social Issues*, ed. George Chryssides (London: Lindsey Press, 2003), p.72.

278 Stephen Kendrick, "Well Being and Being Well", sermon delivered at the First and Second Church in Boston, 1 February 2004; accessed from the website of First and Second Church (www.fscboston.org/sermons.php) on 06/03/05; by permission of the author.

279 Cliff Reed, *Unitarian? What's That?* (London: Lindsey Press, 1999); by permission of the author.

280 Ann Peart, "Of warmth and love and passion: Unitarians and (homo)sexuality", in *Unitarian Perspectives on Contemporary Social Issues*, ed. George Chryssides (London: Lindsey Press, 2003), pp. 61 and 69.

281 James Luther Adams, *The Prophethood of All Believers* (Boston: Beacon Press, 1986), pp. 295-6, 298–303; by permission of the publisher.

282 *Ibid.*, pp. 295-6, 298–303; by permission of the publisher.

283 *What Unitarians Mean By Tolerance* (leaflet) (London: General Assembly of Unitarian and Free Christian Churches, 1998).

284 Ann Peart, "Of warmth and love and passion: Unitarians and (homo)sexuality", in *Unitarian Perspectives on Contemporary Social Issues*, ed. George Chryssides (London: Lindsey Press, 2003), p.72.

285 Tony Cann and George Chryssides, "Unitarians and the Internet", *ibid.*, pp. 124, 125-6.

286 Quoted by William J. Doherty, "Time to commit", *UU World*, January/February 2005 (www.uuworld.org/2005/01/feature3.html), accessed 24/1/05.

287 William J. Doherty, "Time to Commit", *UU World*, January/February 2005 (http://www.uuworld.org/2005/01/feature3.html) accessed 24/1/05; by permission of the author.

288 2005 General Assembly of the Unitarian Universalist Association of Congregations, Fort Worth, Texas website (http://www.uua.org/ga/); accessed 12/3/05; by permission of the UUA.

289 George N. Marshall, *Challenge of a Liberal Faith*, 3rd ed. (Boston: Skinner House Books, 1991), pp. 149–150; by permission of the publisher.

290 Jane Howarth, "Unitarians and penal affairs: values, principles, and action", in *Unitarian Perspectives on Contemporary Social Issues* ed. George Chryssides (London: Lindsey Press, 2003), p.28.

291 Thandeka, "The legacy of caring" in *Singing The Living Tradition* (Boston: Unitarian Universalist Association, 1993), reading 666; by permission of the author.

292 James Luther Adams, *The Prophethood of All Believers* (Boston: Beacon Press, 1986), pp. 152–53; by permission of the publisher.

293 Tom Owen-Towle, *Freethinking Mystics With Hands: Exploring the Heart of Unitarian Universalism* (Boston: Skinner House Books, 1998), p.47; by permission of Tom Owen-Towle.

294 John Clifford, "A Universalist Sense of Ministry", GA Anniversary Sermon, April 2003, Unitarian GA website (www.unitarian.org.uk/anniv_serm003.htm), accessed 30/1/05; by permission of the author.

295 Brenda Wong, ed., *Quotations from the Wayside* (Boston: Skinner House Books, 1999), 41.

296 *Ibid.*, p.41.

297 *Ibid.*, p. 66; by permission of the publisher.

298 George Paxton, "Can war be abolished?" in *Unitarian Perspectives on Contemporary Social Issues,* ed. George Chryssides (London: Lindsey Press, 2003), p.80.

299 Peter Hawkins, "Post-modernism and religion", in *Unitarian Perspectives on Contemporary Religious Thought,* ed. George D. Chryssides (London: Lindsey Press, 1999), p.41.

300 E. H. Chapin, "Moral aspects of city life" (1853) in *Universalism in America: A Documentary History of a Liberal Faith*, 3rd ed., ed. Ernest Cassara (Boston: Skinner House Books, 1997), p.208.

301 Fredric John Muir, *A Reason For Hope: Liberation Theology Confronts A Liberal Faith* (Carmel, CA: Sunflower Ink, 1994), pp. 50–51, 53, 54, 55; by permission of the author.

302 *Singing The Living Tradition* (Boston: Unitarian Universalist Association, 1993), reading 457.

303 The Letter of James 1: 22, 2: 8, 14 –18, New Revised Standard Version of the Bible: Anglicized Edition.

304 Christine Hayhurst, "Making vision work" in *Prospects for the Unitarian Movement*, ed. Matthew F. Smith (London: Lindsey Press, 2002), p.46.

305 James Luther Adams, *The Prophethood of All Believers* (Boston: Beacon Press, 1986), p.23; by permission of the publisher.

306 Emily Howard Jennings Stowe, "The century of the woman movement", from speech to Toronto's Women's Literary Club, 1878, in *Standing Before Us: Unitarian Universalist Women and Social Reform, 1776 – 1936,* ed. Dorothy May Emerson (Boston: Skinner House Books, 2000), p.75.

307 Brenda Wong, ed., *Quotations from the Wayside* (Boston: Skinner House Books, 1999), p.15.

308 *Ibid.,* p.19.

309 Tom Owen-Towle, *Freethinking Mystics With Hands: Exploring the Heart of Unitarian Universalism* (Boston: Skinner House Books, 1998), p.63; by permission of the author.

310 Readings from "The Higher Life" (1908), three sermons by Gertrude von Petzold, from the Hibbert Assembly website (www.hibbert-assembly.org.uk/womenswork/extracts.htm), accessed 28/2/05.

311 Fredric John Muir, *A Reason For Hope: Liberation Theology Confronts A Liberal Faith* (Carmel, CA: Sunflower Ink, 1994), p.61; by permission of the publisher.

312 Melanie Prideaux, "A Unitarian perspective on school education" in *Unitarian Perspectives on Contemporary Social Issues,* ed. George Chryssides (London: Lindsey Press, 2003), p.41.

313 "A Social Program", Report of the National Commission of the Universalist Church (1917) in *Universalism in America: A Documentary History of a Liberal Faith,* 3rd edition, ed. Ernest Cassara (Boston: Skinner House Books, 1997), p.250.

314 Micah 6: 8, New Revised Standard Version of the Bible: Anglicized Edition.

315 Brenda Wong, ed., *Quotations from the Wayside* (Boston: Skinner House Books, 1999), p.37.

316 *Ibid.,* p.55.

317 George Paxton, "Can war be abolished?" in *Unitarian Perspectives on Contemporary Social Issues,* ed. George Chryssides (London: Lindsey Press, 2003), p.79.

318 Tom Owen-Towle, *Freethinking Mystics With Hands: Exploring the Heart of Unitarian Universalism* (Boston: Skinner House Books, 1998), p.49; by permission of the author.

319 From a pastoral message from the Rev. William G. Sinkford, President, Unitarian Universalist Association, 14 January 2005. (www.uua.org/president/050115_king.html) accessed 21/1/05; by permission of the UUA.

320 E. H. Chapin, "Moral aspects of city life" (1853) in *Universalism in America: A Documentary History of a Liberal Faith,* 3rd edition, ed. Ernest Cassara (Boston: Skinner House Books, 1997), pp. 206–7.

321 Mary Wollstonecraft, *Vindication of the Rights of Woman* (Harmondsworth, Middlesex: Penguin Books, 1975), p.252.

322 Tom Owen-Towle, *Freethinking Mystics With Hands: Exploring the Heart of Unitarian Universalism* (Boston: Skinner House Books, 1998), p.59; by permission of the author.

323 Matt Grant, "Clash of civilisations? A Unitarian Christian response", *The Unitarian Christian Herald,* No 55, Autumn 2004; by permission of the author.

324 Cliff Reed, *Unitarian? What's That?* (London: Lindsey Press, 1999); by permission of the author.

325 Paula Cole Jones, "Reconciliation as a spiritual discipline", *UU World,* March/April 2004; by permission of the author.

326 From the Hibbert Assembly Website (www.hibbert-assembly.org.uk/Servetus/reedservetus.htm), accessed 13/2/05.

327 Imre Gellérd, *A History of Transylvanian Unitarianism through Four Centuries of Sermons*, trans. Judit Gellérd (Chico, CA: Uniquest, 1999), p.75; by permission of the author's estate.

328 John A. Buehrens and Forrest Church, *A Chosen Faith: An Introduction to Unitarian Universalism* (Boston: Beacon Press, 1998), p.41.

329 *Ibid.*, p. 168; by permission of the publisher.

330 From the Hibbert Assembly website (www.hibbert-assembly.org.uk/Priestley/quotes.htm), accessed 28.03.05.

331 Brenda Wong, ed., *Quotations from the Wayside*; by permission of the publisher.

332 From Tom Owen-Towle, *The Gospel of Universalism: Hope, Courage, and the Love of God* (Boston: Skinner House Books, 1993), p.22; by permission of the publisher.

333 John A. Buehrens and Forrest Church, *A Chosen Faith: An Introduction to Unitarian Universalism* (Boston: Beacon Press, 1998), p.168; by permission of the publisher.

334 Imre Gellérd, *A History of Transylvanian Unitarianism through Four Centuries of Sermons*, trans. Judit Gellérd (Chico, CA: Uniquest, 1999), p.46; by permission of the author's estate.

335 Francis Power Cobbe, "To an audience of ladies", London, 1881, in *Standing Before Us: Unitarian Universalist Women and Social Reform, 1776 – 1936*, ed. Dorothy May Emerson (Boston: Skinner House Books, 2000), p.91.

336 Forrest Church, ed., *Without Apology: Collected Meditations on Liberal Religion by A. Powell Davies* (Boston: Skinner House Books, 1998), p.93; by permission of the publisher.

337 Quoted by Christine Hayhurst, "Making vision work" in *Prospects for the Unitarian Movement*, ed. Matthew Smith (London: Lindsey Press, 2002), p.46.

Printed in the United Kingdom
by Lightning Source UK Ltd.
130332UK00001B/82-132/P